Streets of Birmingham's Transport

Malcolm Keeley
and Roger Torode
on behalf of Transport Museum Wythall and The Bus Archive

Capital Transport

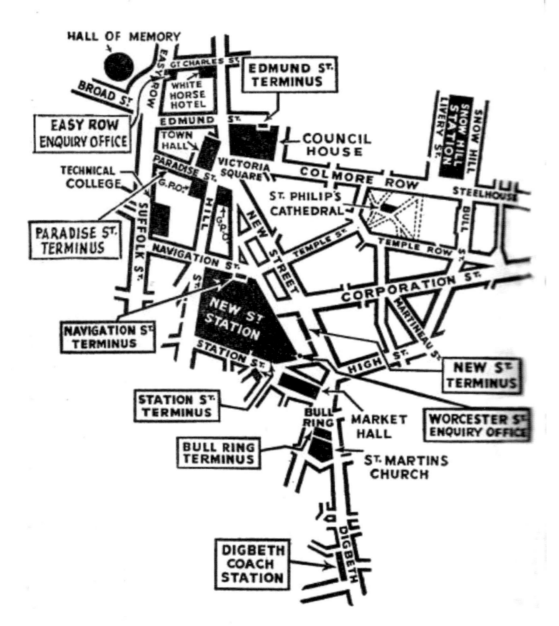

MIDLAND RED BUS DEPARTURE POINTS

First published 2022

ISBN 978 1 85414 466 9

Published by Capital Transport Publishing Ltd
www.capitaltransport.com

Printed by Parksons Graphics

Contents

A Midland Red wartime Daimler pauses in Corporation Street, opposite Lewis's department store. The Lewis's building is still with us although in multiple occupancy but those behind the Daimler are long gone. 2515 was a 1943 CWA6 model with a Duple body; after rebuilding one itself Midland Red had the austerity bodies on the rest of its wartime Daimlers refurbished and modernised by Willowbrook in 1950-1 as seen here, retaining this bus until 1956. *Transport Museum Wythall*

Introduction

We begin with the story of the young lad, lounging on the grass outside a Birmingham pub, his eyes fixed in one direction. Poor mite, was he watching the pub door, waiting for his parents to reel out, hopelessly the worse for drink? No, he was watching the curve in the road for the next bus to arrive; his parents were either at home, blamelessly sober half a mile away, or at work in those days of limited time off.

We are outside the Baldwin in Hall Green during the mid-1950s, the lad basking in the wonderful infinity of school summer holidays. Everlasting sunshine enjoyed with the almost total absence of grown-ups – just make sure you're home for tea. No electronic gadgets, only the powers of curiosity and imagination.

The young lad had noticed that the Birmingham City Transport buses were of different makes and types, with different sounds. Even the ones without a maker's name on their fluted radiators varied. No fleet lists then, it would be some time before he discovered these were Daimlers with AEC, Gardner or Daimler's own engines. The Baldwin was a good spot; it was the terminus of the mighty 29A service which ran across the city, worked by four garages with a wide selection of types such as Crossleys and Leylands. The round journey was 26.7 miles so it was around 140 minutes before the same buses returned. The lad noticed each had handsome gold fleet numbers and he began to memorise them to establish the start and finish of each type.

Moseley village has remained remarkably unchanged from steam tram days. A City of Birmingham Tramways Kitson locomotive waits for its passenger trailer to be loaded before continuing towards Kings Heath. The steam tram era ended on most routes, including this one, on 31 December 1906, new tramcars powered by overhead electricity taking over the next day. *Transport Museum Wythall collection*

Nearby was the Stratford Road. The BCT interest was less here; all the buses on the 37 were Daimlers, a different selection from yet another garage. But there were large numbers of red double-deckers with MIDLAND in generously wide gold letters along the sides, working to and from points beyond the city boundary. Some looked new but others appeared very old.

Occasionally an immaculate bus with the proud legend LEYLAND DIESEL on its bonnet side would roll through, wearing a fine mid-blue and cream livery topped off by a gleaming silver roof, quite unlike the matt khaki of the BCT buses. These regal visitors belonged to Stratford Blue which ran around forty vehicles, almost all Leylands. Their tiny discreet destination boxes were crammed with information and you just had time to read they shared with Midland Red the 150 to and from Stratford. Thanks to good education, the lad knew the town was famous for playwright William Shakespeare. Gosh, Bill must ride these buses between grand feasts of venison and Henley Ices washed down with the Flowers' Ales so prolifically advertised on the bus sides.

The lad in question, of course, is one of your writers, not quite in Shakespeare's league unfortunately. There were other lads (no girls apparently) all over Birmingham gathering slightly different memories. Many of their BCT buses were Guys with loud exhausts blasting up the hills of the great city. These lads may have been in the right corner of town to see the buses of West Bromwich Corporation in their genteel, fully lined-out, livery – well maintained but often in need of a repaint. Or perhaps Walsall Corporation, whose cheaply specified buses almost certainly looked dilapidated in consequence. Kingstanding's kids could see Harper Brothers' buses, what a treat! It would be 1965 before Harpers reached the city centre and we could share the joy!

We are delighted that the publisher has asked us to assemble this collection of Birmingham bus and tram photographs, covering all the major stage carriage operators in the city as well as the few areas regularly travelled by BCT's vehicles outside the boundary. An earlier book published by Capital Transport, 'Birmingham by Bus' by Malcolm Keeley and Derek Potter, covered the 1960s and '70s in colour. This is a black & white album which allows us an earlier time frame. Older photos accompany a first section describing the growth of the city. The rest of the book covers the city geographically from the end of World War Two until the finish of BCT in 1969. First we wander around the city centre, taking in the huge changes, and then tour the suburbs in an anti-clockwise direction before leaving the city via West Bromwich.

To avoid captions becoming over-complicated, we have endeavoured to simplify the vehicle descriptions. Unless otherwise stated, all the Birmingham Daimlers and Guys have Metro-Cammell bodies, while the Crossleys are complete products from the Stockport factory.

We thank the many photographers for their fine work. They will have their own heroes but most acknowledge the late Fred York as among the finest and this book is a tribute to his perseverance. Fred followed in the footsteps of pictorial pioneers like W A ("Cam") Camwell who endeavoured to include sufficient background to identify the location. Fred notably walked around the Inner Circle in the late 1950s, recording the major changes occurring along the route, as well as covering the rest of the city superbly.

Particular thanks to The Transport Museum Wythall for access to its archives which happily include most of Fred York's local pictures as well as many other photographers' work. Similar thanks to The Bus Archive which protects the negatives of many more fine photographers. The Transport Museum Wythall can also offer you the most superb collections of preserved Birmingham City Transport and Midland Red buses, plus those of other operators. The fine work of these organisations deserves every support.

Individuals that have assisted the writers, usually by answering questions about sixty or more years ago, include David Barber, John Carroll, Phil Drake, Andrew Gardner, Paul Gray, Peter Jaques and Monty Russell. Thanks too to people like Barry Ware who over many years have trickled wonderful facts and stories into the writers' ears that now add extra interest to the captions. Apologies to those not mentioned - there must be many!

Malcolm Keeley and Roger Torode
April 2022.

The City of Birmingham Tramways Co Ltd deserves the credit for the first overhead electric trams in the city, in May 1901 along the Bristol Road. CBT became part of the British Electric Traction (BET) in June 1902. Electric trams were soon introduced between the city centre along the Pershore Road, reaching their ultimate destination at Cotteridge by June 1904. CBT 242, built that year at Kyotts Lake Road Works, is seen at the Cotteridge terminus at the junction of Pershore Road and Watford Road. Many 4-wheel tramcars similar to this passed to BCT in 1911-2, CBT 242 becoming BCT 472. Most of the ex-CBT cars were improved with top covers and platform vestibules by BCT in the 1920s. *Richard Stevenson collection*

This scoop line-up in Edmund Street on 2 May 1939 shows the development of Birmingham's trams. No 53 belonged to 1905-8 batches of short wheelbase four-wheel three-window UEC-bodied Brill tramcars, originally open-top but later fitted with top covers. The short tramcars were able to handle the tight clearances on the curves of the twisting and hilly 32 route through the Jewellery Quarter to Winson Green. Those used on the 32 were fitted with Maley track brakes after a fatal runaway accident in 1907 and bow collectors replaced the usual trolley poles in the mid-1920s. The Dudley Road services had been a stronghold of the 71-220 class but behind no 53, and working as far as Grove Lane (tram route number 55), is no 334, one of the 301 class briefly operated on this corridor, having been displaced from Selly Oak by bogie cars released by the Soho Road conversion. Finally bogie car 634 graces the Dudley Road on a short to Windmill Lane (30). *R T Coxon/ Transport Museum Wythall*

Public transport and the growing city

Birmingham was known as 'The Workshop of the World', achieving its success by avoiding dependency on one industry. Prosperity came through the thousand trades the city was famous for and the versatile Brummie craftsmen's ability to move between them. The city has more canals than Venice, in earlier times bringing in coal from South Staffordshire to feed the metal based trades with gun and jewellery quarters famously evolving. Parts of the town became overcrowded and unwholesome; thankfully some of the worst old slums were removed through the construction of New Street and Snow Hill stations, making Birmingham a centre of the national railway network. This was followed by Joseph Chamberlain's 'Great Improvement Scheme', the new Corporation Street (1878-82) slicing through more bad housing.

Many of the city's outlying districts were originally quite separate rural villages or hamlets. In the second half of the 19th century, businessmen and prosperous artisans followed new railway lines to areas such as Acock's Green, Balsall Heath, Cotteridge, Erdington and Gravelly Hill, Selly Oak, Stechford and Yardley. Suburbs began with modest houses with small gardens in the fresh air away from the city's industries. Some areas were particularly distinctive and have managed to remain so to this day. The Cadburys made the move to undeveloped land in Bournville in 1879 for their subsequently world-famous chocolate factory. Fourteen years later they bought adjacent land to build good quality homes with gardens and hedges for their workers, influencing town planning not only in Birmingham and encouraging future garden cities.

These new areas began to be linked by horse buses and, where patronage repaid the cost, horse-drawn tramways. Horses proved inadequate for busy corridors and began to give way to steam tramway engines in the 1880s. Birmingham also experimented with battery and cable cars. Electricity was thought to be the way forward and from 1897 the British Electric Traction Co Ltd (BET) aspired to purchase all the tramways in the region and electrify them. Some of the local authorities, however, decided to purchase and operate the trams in their area themselves, including Birmingham which took them over upon expiry of the various leases that had been granted to the private operators. From 1904 route after route came under Corporation control and was electrified, and additional new routes were introduced.

Birmingham achieved city status in 1889. Many neighbouring authorities now contained densely populated districts and had effectively become suburbs of Birmingham. A series of boundary extensions began with Harborne, Balsall Heath, Saltley and Ward End added to the city in 1891. Residential infilling was occurring around the city. The Greater Birmingham Scheme in 1911 unified many more of the neighbouring authorities into the city, now trebled in size. Included were Yardley, Handsworth and King's Norton, old parishes of considerable size with plenty of rural land that would soon be developed.

BET concentrated its horse and motor bus operations into one company, the Birmingham & Midland Motor Omnibus Co Ltd (BMMO for short). Birmingham Corporation would not allow omnibus services to compete with its tramways. As the electric tram network expanded vigorously, BMMO was obliged to withdraw its facilities. Conflict with BMMO, which became better known as Midland 'Red', seemed inevitable. Instead in 1914 BCT and BMMO entered into a classic agreement whereby BMMO continued to operate services between Birmingham and places outside the city boundary, leaving city services entirely to BCT. The latter agreed to restrict its activities to inside the boundary and not compete outside. This agreement resulted in happy relations until PTE days and, as will be seen, there were a couple of interesting exceptions allowing BCT vehicles beyond the western boundary.

Birmingham had strong demands along corridors radiating from the centre and could justify some superb tramway improvements in the 1920s such as tracks along centre reservations, ideal for high-speed running. Such progress was impossible in the Black Country with its small villages giving rise to complicated and comparatively low passenger demands, and narrow roads causing many single track sections. Bus design was improving, competition began and the Black Country tramway network, operated by the privately owned BET, began to unravel.

Next door to Birmingham in West Bromwich, the South Staffordshire Tramways lease covering the routes between Birmingham via West Bromwich to Dudley and Wednesbury expired in 1924. West Bromwich wanted change and a 15-year operating agreement was reached with Birmingham Corporation Tramways to run the mileage instead.

BET shook off its remaining tramway responsibilities; moving investment towards its bus-operating Midland Red subsidiary. From 1928 Birmingham Corporation trams took over from BET subsidiary Birmingham District Tramways on the Birmingham – Smethwick – Oldbury – Dudley corridor. The last BET-operated trams in the Black Country ran on 30 September 1930.

Buses were distinctly improving with smoother engines, better seating and pneumatic tyres so trams began to be replaced in Birmingham too from the early 1930s. The economics were turning against trams which needed a population density high enough to justify the cost of the permanent way. Inner area populations thinned as slums were replaced by new housing estates built on the outskirts of the city. Trams had been previously regarded as essential to meet dense demands but buses had proved themselves on the Outer and Inner Circles, the latter in particular busier than many tram routes.

For the first major conversion, along the Coventry Road in January 1934, the replacement vehicles were trolleybuses but all subsequent conversions used motorbuses. The tramways through West Bromwich were replaced in April 1939 by buses operated by both Birmingham and West Bromwich Corporations. The tramcars to Dudley via Oldbury were replaced by motorbuses in October 1939. The various local authorities outside Birmingham along the route had agreed that Midland Red buses should replace the tramways on their behalves. The replacing bus

One of the pioneer motor buses in Birmingham is seen on the Hagley Road. It was a Brush B-type new in 1906 to the Birmingham & Midland Motor Omnibus Company, soon to be better known as Midland 'Red'. The early motor buses were soon withdrawn from Birmingham and horse buses returned for the time being. *Richard Stevenson collection*

The BET owned tramways in Worcester and Kidderminster also developed bus services. Worcester Electric Traction ran its holly green and cream buses as far north as Rubery where 1913 Daimler 40 hp FK 412 is seen at the Rose & Crown. The Worcester and Kidderminster bus operations led to the formation in August 1914 of the Worcestershire Motor Transport Co Ltd. This was short-lived as World War One enveloped the country and at least the chassis of the Worcestershire buses, which all had orthodox gearbox drive, were taken by the military. Fellow BET subsidiary BMMO (Midland Red) at that time favoured Tilling-Stevens buses with petrol-electric transmission, a design disliked by the military. BMMO took over the Worcestershire operations in November 1914, the Rubery service being subsumed into its Birmingham – Malvern service. Some of Worcestershire's bodies survived to be fitted to BMMO Tilling-Stevens chassis. In the background is one of Birmingham Corporation Tramways' first ten motorbuses, delivered in 1913, on its service to the tram terminus at Selly Oak. Extensions of the Bristol Road tram route to Rednal and Rubery were planned and the ten Daimlers were purchased for this task until the work was achieved. World War One and its economic aftermath caused considerable delay, trams not reaching Rubery until February 1926. The Daimlers were numbered 1-10 and carried registrations OA 1601-10. They did not last for long in this form, however, as the Daimler chassis were also taken by the military for World War One. The bodies and registration numbers OA 1601-10 were transferred to new Tilling-Stevens chassis in 1915. *Richard Stevenson collection*

services were thus jointly operated although in practice they reverted to the pre-1928 pattern with BCT vehicles generally working the Bearwood and Soho journeys, and company vehicles running to Dudley.

The City Council already had grand plans for the city before the outbreak of World War Two in 1939. The war damaged the city but the inability to progress its plans meant decay which may have proved even more serious. Buses and trams, like much of the machinery the city depended on for its wealth, were both over-used and under-maintained during World War Two. By the end of it, everything was in a run-down state.

The war, however, did give time for reflection. The ambitious reconstruction plans for the city centre, roads and slum clearance were honed. Immediately after the war, the City Council applied to the Ministry of Town and Country Planning for a compulsory purchase order covering five central redevelopment areas with housing segregated from industry, namely Duddeston & Nechells, Newtown, Highgate, Lee Bank and Ladywood. This was approved in June 1947 but progress was initially slow. The economic state of the country with shortages of labour and materials meant it was well into the 1950s before schemes began to come into fruition.

A major problem was building land. If homes were to be demolished in the central area, the people had to be rehoused. Birmingham had continued to expand its boundaries until 1931. The years between the two World Wars had seen the construction of attractive but sprawling low density housing estates, following the influence of families like the Cadburys. Farmland was overtaken by completely new suburbs such as Hall Green and Sheldon. Huge municipal housing estates, such as Kingstanding, Weoley Castle, Fox Hollies and Gospel Farm, were notable for their circles, ovals and crescents to avoid the monotony of the earlier streets. Neighbouring local authorities strengthened their opposition to the big city's unrestricted growth. Even Birmingham was accepting that land was being developed that was too distant from the city centre. Residents were now living up to seven miles from the centre and grumbled about long travel times while the Transport Department, now the largest municipal transport undertaking in the country, complained that the distant low density estates and a policy of cheap fares for workers were causing financial losses.

The final conversions to buses were the Bristol Road services in July 1952 and the Aston Road group in July 1953. These tram routes had long sections of reserved track but, without investment, not enough to warrant retaining the paraphernalia surrounding tramway operation and maintenance. The Bristol Road was considered by tramway supporters to be a showpiece route but it suffered congestion through Selly Oak and Northfield while the Pershore Road branch offered little opportunity for a modern tramway. Significant tramway development had stopped in 1928, ideally branches needed to have been added in the early 1930s into the new estates at Weoley Castle and Allen's Cross.

The land in the pre-1931 boundary extensions was soon built over. Birmingham City Council concentrated on public housing after World War Two which, after the development of Tile Cross, were built to higher densities than before, including tower blocks. Middle-class commuter suburbs for private ownership were thus constructed outside the city in areas like Solihull and Sutton Coldfield and these communities defended their areas from annexation by Birmingham. The agreement with Midland Red meant these areas were served by the company which consequently undertook many revisions to its route network.

Building land over the boundary in Warwickshire was purchased by the city from a private builder to create Kingshurst from 1953. This was also extra business for Midland Red. The purchase of Castle Bromwich airfield in 1959 would lead to Castle Vale which could be served by Birmingham City Transport buses.

The city centre was hugely affected by the construction of the inner ring road which commenced in 1957. Initially known as the Ringway, it was completed in 1971 when the tunnel under Paradise Circus was opened and HM Queen Elizabeth II christened the whole ring road Queensway. The Aston Expressway was opened in 1972, placing the city at the centre of the country's motorway network, but its construction virtually destroyed the Aston area.

With the conurbation already considered big enough, the idea grew of satellite towns some distance away beyond a green belt. New towns for Birmingham's population overspill were announced for the future Telford, near Dawley, in 1962 and Redditch in 1963. In 1964 the new Labour administration gave Birmingham permission to build outside the boundary at Chelmsley Wood and things really got moving from 1967. Almost all the five central renewal areas had been cleared and redeveloped by the time Birmingham City Transport ended in 1969. Chelmsley Wood, being outside the city, was in the Midland Red area.

Birmingham City Council considered itself to be large enough to be efficient, and distinct from the rest of the conurbation. Although it needed some additional land, ambitions to expand in any major way into neighbouring authority areas had long disappeared. The same view applied to its Transport Department. Birmingham City Transport was as keen as mustard to protect its own territory but anyone claiming that the West Midlands Passenger Transport Executive was a takeover by BCT is wide of the mark. It was the national Labour Party that created the PTE whose top layer of management was almost entirely non-BCT. Although its vehicles ran by agreement to West Bromwich, Dudley and Wednesbury, there is no evidence that BCT ever really aspired to operate anywhere other than Brum – which it served really well.

This book ends with the demise of Birmingham City Transport in 1969, along with the municipal buses of Walsall, West Bromwich and Wolverhampton. Coventry's buses followed later as did the local services of Midland Red. The handover of these buses to the West Midlands PTE proved to be a forerunner of bigger things to come. Local government reorganisation in 1974 saw the creation of a West Midlands county. Birmingham was to be enlarged to include Solihull and Sutton Coldfield. Solihull remained independent but Sutton Coldfield became part of Birmingham from April 1974.

THE TERMINUS

PRIORY RD. HALL GREEN

Opposite top: The Bristol Road was regarded as the showpiece of the tramway system, including the fabulous turning circle at Rednal set against the backdrop of the Lickey Hills, a huge area of recreational land made available with the assistance of the Cadbury family. This was a terminus with real elegance, even after the shortages of war as seen here. There was a huge shelter to accommodate the bank holiday throngs of returning passengers queueing around the tram terminus loop. Things look a bit quieter as 589, 590 and 604 await return to the city centre. These larger bogie cars were the standard Birmingham purchase from 1913. Although top-covered, 512-636 were the last trams delivered with open upper deck vestibules, these being enclosed between 1926 and 1931. *S J Butler (G H F Atkins collection)*

Opposite: Birmingham's first trolleybuses entered service in November 1922 on the Nechells service. The tramway track needed relaying so the Transport Committee thought it a "suitable occasion for an experiment to be made with railless trolley vehicles", the route pioneering tram to trolleybus conversions in the UK. The new vehicles had "the top seats protected from the weather as in tramway practice". This was revolutionary at the time for double-deck buses and Birmingham became the first city to extend the concept to motorbuses two years later. Trolleybuses 1-12 had Railless chassis, 51-seat bodies by Charles H Roe and were operated by Washwood Heath depot; no 8 turns off Washwood Heath Road through the depot gates when new. It looks incredibly narrow, which it was by modern standards, but the effect is exacerbated by its height, just short of 5 metres (well over 16 feet). This original generation was replaced in 1932 by new Leylands that looked like motor buses. The Nechells trolleybuses were suddenly replaced by motor buses after 30 September 1940. Trolleybuses returning to the depot via the tram route had to trail a metal skate along the tram rail for the electrical return. This caused unacceptable flashing under wartime blackout regulations. Apparently only a temporary suspension, in practice trolleybuses never returned to Nechells. *Transport Museum Wythall collection*

Above: Yardley was transferred from Worcestershire to the city in the great expansion of boundaries in 1911. The pre-1911 Yardley parish covered quite a large area, hence the name Yardley Wood although the latter is some distance away from what is regarded as Yardley today. Housing development began encroaching in the early 1920s on Trittiford Farm (earlier spellings include Titterford). Serving still partially rural areas could be difficult. A nearby bus facility was the Yardley Wood Road 13 service from the city centre. It was not until June 1929, after a ford had been bridged in Yardley Wood Road and some road widening, that many journeys could be extended via Pendeen Road and Glastonbury Road as service 13A to this new terminus outside Trittiford Park. 1927 ADC 507 no 254 (OX 1520) shares the attractive view along Priory Road towards Shirley; the road was subsequently widened to dual carriageway as far as the boundary. The 13 and associated service 24 to Warstock were worked by Acocks Green garage until Yardley Wood opened in November 1938. The 13A was rerouted in September 1939 to run directly via Trittiford Road to this point. *Commercial postcard*

The Corporation bus fleet's traffic requirement had grown by February 1929 to 221 plus 10% maintenance spare. The first 30 AEC Regents were delivered the same year (338-67). The modern-looking chassis design with powerful six-cylinder petrol engine was a major advance while the bodies moved ahead in several respects, notably the enclosed staircases. Further AEC Regent contracts followed, bus 397 in Dulverton Road, Witton helps to clear demand from the GEC works and offices. The Regents were among the first Birmingham buses to have roller destination blinds but were only able to show around 25 different displays (post-war buses could show up to 60 destinations). 397 will be working around the Outer Circle, hence the Perry Barr display; the blind is unable to show its actual final destination at Soho Road so this has to be carried on the supplementary board.
Transport Museum Wythall collection

A stunning view of AEC Q demonstrator AHX 63, loading at Five Ways before proceeding along Calthorpe Road. In the background are Victorian shops in Hagley Road on the left and Broad Street on the right. It is believed the body was built by London General; it had many design details common with London trolleybus 61. It ran as an AEC demonstrator for Birmingham in 1933-4, carrying fleet number 93. It was then converted from petrol to diesel and returned to Birmingham in 1935, being bought by the transport department later that year. It was originally painted in this variation of Birmingham's colours. BCT's style of livery with cream upper works was considered out-of-date by 1930, only Oldham Corporation also staying with it. It came back into fashion in the 1960s, Eire's state operator CIE paying the livery the greatest compliment of imitation, adopting it for its double-deck fleet, initially even with the khaki roof. *AEC*

When Midland Red began to build up its network of services from central Birmingham to points outside the city boundary, the first daily route was to Walsall, commenced on Christmas Eve 1913. This route received the 118 identification in the company's 1928 renumbering of its services and, in the good years, the full route operated around every six minutes. There were numerous short workings, notably the 119 between central Birmingham and the Scott Arms, Great Barr which became entirely within Birmingham following extension of the city boundary in 1928 when Perry Barr was incorporated from Staffordshire. This meant there were residents served only by Midland Red services operating entirely within the Birmingham city boundary but outside the 1914 agreement. By a further agreement the services continued to be run by the company on behalf of Birmingham Corporation until the anomaly was addressed in the late 1950s. This is the Scott Arms stop for buses towards the city centre, complete with a classic Birmingham cast stop column and 'lollipop' round stop plate. This pre-war picture shows a real Midland Red rarity. EHA 297 was one of three Brush-bodied FEDD-type buses built in 1938 with full width cabs. Intended to look more streamlined, they no doubt caused annoyance whenever attention to engines was required so they were rebuilt to half cab in 1940. *Transport Museum Wythall collection*

Photographs 1946-1969: A Walk around Town

For several centuries Birmingham was basically one road from Deritend to Dale End plus side streets. It was possible to cross the River Rea at Deritend and a four arch bridge was built there in the 17th century. Today the river in its culvert can just be glimpsed from the top deck of buses. Digbeth and High Street Deritend are thus among the oldest thoroughfares in the city and were once Tudor in character. The Old Crown in High Street Deritend is reputed to date from 1368, although parts are thought to be early 16th century, and is the last half-timbered survivor along this ancient road, having resisted destruction in all the proposals over the years for 'street improvements', not least widening to dual carriageway between 1953 and 1955. Guy 3057 with grille lacking its decorative trims sets down on an inbound journey in August 1969; it would soon be a WMPTE bus. *F W York/ Transport Museum Wythall*

Enthusiasts recording on film the comings and goings at Midland Red's Digbeth Coach Station would keep their eyes open for other buses of interest. 3103, working from Acocks Green garage, was one of three assorted experimental lightweight buses received by Birmingham City Transport in 1952-4. It was based on an ordinary Daimler CVG6 chassis so all the weight saving was in the body built by Crossley. This appeared to be influenced by Midland Red's latest D7 buses which, on the upper deck, also had double deflector vents in the front windows and pivoted extraction vents on the side rear windows. *Transport Museum Wythall*

While other major junctions received massive flyovers and underpasses, a 'temporary' prefabricated flyover was built to take traffic out of the city from High Street Deritend into Camp Hill over the inbound traffic from Coventry Road. The flyover was assembled very quickly. Here, on 13 October 1961, the first piece is in place and Dodge trucks are in attendance. A Midland Red Leyland and BCT Daimler CVD6 2660 are among traffic making their way around the side; two days later they would be going over the top! The flyover was 790 feet long, 10 feet wide and 16 feet 6 inches tall at its highest point. It was finally removed in 1986 and reverted to a simple junction, largely thanks to construction of the nearby Middleway. *David Barber collection*

Light loadings were not unusual on the service between the airport and the city centre. BCT replaced its single-deck fleet with new Leylands in 1950, most being Weymann-bodied PS2 Tigers like 2260 here in Digbeth. *Transport Museum Wythall*

Midland Red's Birmingham - Coventry service, commenced in February 1914, was the longest of its early routes at 18 miles. In those early days, it took 80 minutes in each direction but the 159, as it was eventually numbered, became speedily timed at 58 minutes (with only 2 minutes at each terminus), aided from the 1950s onward by the dual carriageway along the A45. Today's limited stop timings are closer to the 1914 era. FEDD 2264 nears journey's end on Digbeth, passing the junction with Meriden Street, appropriate as the 159 served Meriden, the alleged centre of England. The bulk of the demand within the city boundary would have been handled by buses like BCT's Daimler CVD6 1840, following on the 60 from Cranes Park. The Brush bodies of the 1938-9 FEDDs needed major rebuilding after World War Two but, as can be seen, 2264 only received visible attention to its lower deck. *Transport Museum Wythall*

The trams and replacing buses to Bordesley Green and Stechford offered passengers two routes out of the city centre. The more obvious of these was via Digbeth, Deritend, Bordesley, Coventry Road and Cattell Road. The widening of Digbeth and Deritend to dual carriageway was proposed for 1940, requiring the replacement of the Stechford trams by new bus services numbered 53 and 54. World War Two stalled that proposal and the tram conversion was delayed until 1948. The other Stechford service turned off Digbeth at Meriden Street and took a 'back route' via Fazeley Street, Great Barr Street and Garrison Lane to reach Bordesley Green; 1949 Daimler CVD6 1979 was seen on Fazeley Street in February 1957. The peak vehicle requirement on the 53/54 services before any journeys were extended beyond Stechford was 30, plus maintenance spares. *F W York/ Transport Museum Wythall*

This is the steady incline up Digbeth leading to St Martin's Church and the Bull Ring. A policeman strides back to his station located just off-camera on the right. Birmingham's first Leyland PD2 to be delivered with Brush's interpretation of the department's standard body design waits for the traffic lights to change. 1656 entered service in March 1948 during the brief time that grab rails were favoured across the front windows instead of below them; 1657-1755 had them in the lower position. *Geoff Kelland/ MRK collection*

The Bull Ring was once the village green and markets began in the 12th century. Midland Red's buses to destinations south-east of Birmingham loaded alongside St Martin's-in-the-Bull Ring from 1914 until preparations for the new Bull Ring began almost half a century later. Among the Midland Reds was the occasional Stratford Blue. Midland Red shared the old 150 between Birmingham and Stratford upon Avon with its subsidiary Stratford Blue for nearly 20 years from 1952 upon increasing the frequency from hourly to half-hourly. Stratford Blue initially used its latest PD2/12 models with Leyland bodies, 23-5 (MAC 570-2), but in 1956 a further three PD2/12s were delivered and regularly used on the service. Leyland had ceased bodybuilding so the bodies were by Willowbrook which was a favoured supplier to Stratford Blue from 1950 onwards. No 20 (TNX 454) is seen loading in the Bull Ring in May 1956, with a good view along Moor Street. A Midland Red LD8 class stands behind. *S J Butler (G H F Atkins collection)*

The first big conversion from trams occurred in January 1934 when the Coventry Road route was converted with 50 Leyland trolleybuses with Metro-Cammell bodies. The Leylands no doubt added to their appeal by having traction equipment by local manufacturer GEC, attractive at a desperate economic time for the city. The trolleybuses were successful but the Transport Department decided motor buses would be even more suitable for subsequent conversions. The Coventry Road trolleybuses were retained until July 1951. Trolleybus 27 approaches the end of Moor Street and will turn left at the Bull Ring towards Digbeth. Confusingly motorbuses duplicated the fleet numbers of the tramcars and then the trolleybuses triplicated them! *R T Wilson*

Inner Ring Road construction began in 1957 and the old Moor Street gradually transmogrified into Moor Street Ringway (later renamed Queensway). This part of Moor Street would remain as a slip road off the Ringway being constructed on the left. The driver of Guy Arab/ Metro-Cammell 2569 has to set down passengers at a temporary stop by a pile of rubble in September 1959. On the right is the passenger entrance to Moor Street station, opened by the Great Western Railway in 1909 to relieve congestion at Snow Hill. The GWR station building is a remarkable survivor among all the reconstruction around this area. *F W York/ Transport Museum Wythall*

Work on St Martin's Circus is quite well advanced in this view of Daimler CVD6 2101. To the right is the part of the old Moor Street retained as a slip road. CVD6s 2031-2130 had low fleet numbers for 'New Look' buses. They were half of an existing order for 200 buses placed in 1947. BCT asked for the second 100 to be fitted with the new design fronts. Metro-Cammell accepted the change in December 1948 but it caused delivery to be even further delayed than normal at the time, arriving in 1950-1 alongside Guys 2526-2625. *F W York/ Transport Museum Wythall*

In this view taken during the reconstruction of the Bull Ring, the Midland Red buses have been evicted from the shadow of St Martin's Church although old shops remain. Northbound Daimler CVD6 1767 is finding its way through the construction of St Martin's Circus to reach its next stop in New Street. The cross-city service 29A had been introduced on 1 January 1936. Even though its route through Hall Green differed radically from the existing 29, the Transport Department numbered it 29A in the successful hope that the Chief Constable would not notice it was an extra bus route through the busy Bull Ring! Several of these early CVD6s were added to Hockley's allocation from 1954 after the garage gained a share in the 29/29A.
Transport Museum Wythall

The service vehicle fleet was modernised in 1947-8 with 1934-5 AOG-registered Daimler COG5s whose double-deck bus bodies were worn out. Former Northern Counties-bodied 674 became number 27 in the service vehicle fleet and would be called out to buses in trouble like 1686 on the upward gradient of the Bull Ring. First gear was advisable here although a few drivers thought otherwise on powerful Leylands at the cost of clutch fumes afflicting downstairs passengers or worse. Many of these lorry conversions had long lives, some surviving well into the PTE years. *N S Stone*

The newly constructed part of the Ringway at the back of Marks & Spencers provided a temporary home for Midland Red services formerly terminating alongside St Martin's Church and soon to move into the new Bull Ring Bus Station. Hard to believe there were people who were not particularly fond of Midland Red's own BMMO buses although the D9 model, of which two are seen here, generally melted the hardest hearts. This collection may have had wider appeal, however, as the remaining buses are Leylands with Leyland's own bodywork. Three are 1953 LD8s, built with Midland Red's ideas on frontal design. The odd one out is a Stratford Blue JUE-registered 1950 PD2 on the 150 for its home town. Moor Street has been one of the sections of the Queensway downgraded in recent years. This spot is again an important loading point for buses although identifying the location is hampered as the road network has changed considerably with the latest redevelopment of the Bull Ring. Moor Street now takes a sharp left turn alongside the railway station and the background is dominated by the Selfridges building. *G H Stone*

Shoppers traditionally moved from High Street and New Street, past the Market Hall as the highway broadened out, to the Bull Ring and vice versa. This March 1959 view looks from St Martin's up the hill towards the junction with New Street and High Street at the top. On the left can be seen the tall Doric columns of the Market Hall, built in the 1830s but burnt out during the first concentrated air raid of World War Two on central Birmingham on the night of 25-26 August 1940. Beyond Paul Taylor's premises on the left is Phillips Street, soon to become part of a temporary diversion to reach New Street. The Rotunda was built here. The last big raid was the night of 9-10 April 1941 when the shops on the east side of the Bull Ring and buildings on the corner of New Street and High Street were destroyed. New Street is behind the Bedford S lorry. Redevelopment of the New Street/ High Street site was slow and the replacement buildings would have been very new in this view of Crossley 2465 on loan to Acocks Green garage from Miller Street. Temporary shops had been built on the right but already had been demolished to make way for the inner ring road. The construction of St Martin's Circus badly dislocated the important pedestrian route, condemning them to congested subways, the latest rebuild of the Bull Ring has corrected this. *F W York/ Transport Museum Wythall*

1949 Brush-bodied Leyland PD2 1753 loads in the Bull Ring for Baldwin's Lane, Hall Green around 1953. Alongside are some of the temporary shops built on the blitzed site across the road from the Market Hall, including the fondly remembered Pimms for Pets. Provision for semaphore trafficators was specified for all the early post-war buses, the offside one can be seen just behind the cab door. They now had a hinged arm which permitted them to bend without damage but the mortality of the bulbs remained very high. Flashing indicators became legal in 1954 and the first big test began in September 1955 involving converting a hundred of the newest vehicles between 2901 and 3227. The flashing indicators soon proved their reliability and general retrofitting across the entire fleet began in autumn 1957. *Transport Museum Wythall*

Moving from High Street towards the space once occupied by BCT 2465, on 17th February 1969 Walsall Corporation 56 will find a very different outlook and have to turn left onto St Martin's Circus Ringway. Walsall's General Manager, Ronald Edgley Cox, raised the profile of his transport undertaking by ensuring at least one new bus was exhibited at each Commercial Motor Show. No 56 was the 1968 exhibit and used Daimler's prototype chassis for an order from South Africa. Definitely not a Fleetline, its Cummins V6-200 9.63 litre engine was mounted in the rear offside corner. It was 36 feet long and its 86-seat body was built by Northern Counties in remarkably restrained style for a Walsall show model. It had a second staircase and exit at the extreme rear. The bus was intended to be driver only with activity at the rear door being supervised by an early CCTV system. The latter was extremely unreliable so the bus always ran with a conductor, usually on the 118 service. Its livery was unique, being sky blue and off-white. Surprisingly 56 has survived and is preserved and displayed at Wythall by Dave Taylor. *Malcolm Keeley*

This is the completed rebuilding of the Bull Ring seen in July 1964 from the multi-storey car park constructed opposite St Martins, across St Martins Circus Ringway and up to the Rotunda. It has now been rebuilt again but the Rotunda has gained the affection of Brummies and survives. The driver of Leyland 2165 is enjoying full ventilation while the BMC car transporter is a reminder of the importance of a good road system to Birmingham's component manufacturers. *T W Moore*

One of the earliest production Daimler Fleetlines, Park Royal-bodied 3292, heralds the start of the new order just as surely as the bright lights in the background. Not quite Piccadilly Circus but it's the thought that counts. A memorable feature of the new generation of buses was the sickly yellow ceilings. Their employment upstairs was perhaps understandable to disguise the nicotine stains from the cigarette smoking then allowed in the upper saloon but downstairs they caused a generally oppressive feel. One thinks of the BCT 'Standards', from COG5s to CVG6s via numerous Leylands, Crossleys and Guys, as being in control for decades. Here on the Coventry Road services, only 12 years separated trolleybuses from Fleetlines and similar short periods applied to many of the later tram-to-bus conversions. *T W Moore*

By September 1959 the Ringway works had caused the 29/29A Hall Green to Kingstanding services to be diverted at the top of the Bull Ring and turn left into Phillips Street, running alongside the old Market Hall. The buildings to the left of 1947 Daimler CVA6 1483 had recently been cleared. 1483 is approaching Worcester Street where it will turn right to regain the normal route in New Street. This bus had a serious accident in early life and had to be repaired by Metro-Cammell in June 1948. *F W York/ Transport Museum Wythall*

Above: Worcester Street was a significant thoroughfare although there is virtually nothing left of it today. It ran south from New Street, past the western end of the Market Hall, to a junction with Edgbaston Street, Pershore Street, Smallbrook Street and Dudley Street. Smallbrook Queensway basically follows the alignment of Worcester Street and Smallbrook Street with a curve above the junction of the old roads. Midland Red 1955 D7 4448 has come down Worcester Street from New Street in March 1959. The gables of the shop roofs looked more decorative than practical, at least at this end of the street. At the far end of the gabled shops was number 27, from 1937 Midland Red's principal Booking & Enquiry office in Birmingham. This was also the headquarters of its Long Distance Services Dept. The ground floor dealt with the public while support staff were accommodated in the upper floors, including the Chart Room where all long distance coach bookings had to be carefully recorded in the pre-computer era. *F W York/ Transport Museum Wythall*

Opposite top: This is an interesting picture of work in progress with the line of the future Queensway shaping up between the old buildings. The ruined Market Hall, seen on the left, was originally expected to be retained and the giant gyratory that became St Martin's Circus Queensway was designed to go around it. The southern side of the gyratory followed the line of Bell Street while here the northern side followed Phillips Street. The decision to demolish the Market Hall in favour of further shops and Manzoni Gardens did not amend this proposed road layout. On the right are the doomed gabled shops of Worcester Street. Beyond those is a rounded building standing between Queen's Drive and the beginning of Station Street. 1951 Daimler CVD6 2654 is basically following Phillips Street, the parked van and car are on the actual former alignment, but today's Brummies will recognise the shape of the Queensway where, despite the latest rebuilding, buses still load today at the end of the approach to New Street station. Bus driving could be quite a contrast between the two operators. BCT 2654 will take 20 minutes to reach Stechford, built up all the way, while Midland Red S15 4626's journey to Nottingham will be only 15 minutes short of three hours. *R Mallabon/ Transport Museum Wythall*

Opposite: In the days before the Bull Ring Bus Station opened in 1963, Midland Red services coming into Birmingham via Aston would set down their remaining passengers here in High Street before turning right into New Street to load and return north via Corporation Street. 1752, seen in July 1950, was one of 135 FEDDs built in 1935-6 with robust Metro-Cammell bodies that gave long service without major rebuilding. *Transport Museum Wythall*

Opposite top: As we walk along High Street, on the right we can look into Carrs Lane. Three buses led by no 451 head a line of Villa Park football extras. The driver of 451 is in his seat and an Inspector approaches to despatch the next buses to the loading stop in Dale End. Villa Park was served by trams until the end of 1949, it is possible this is the first time buses handled the crowds. All three are 1929-31 petrol-engined AEC Regents, life extended in wartime (1943-4) with new Brush 'austerity' bodies. Largely to wartime specification, the severe bodies were softened internally by incorporating some of the fixtures and fittings of their original bodies, notably the upholstered seats. Most new wartime buses had to have wooden slatted seats. Clearly visible is the re-used destination gear from the old bodies which had narrower blind apertures than later buses. *S N J White/ The Bus Archive*

Opposite: 3247 of the 1962 evaluation batch of ten Daimler Fleetlines is about to turn right from High Street into Union Street in July 1966. Under the road is the railway tunnel from Snow Hill station. Leyland PD2 1755, with Brush body, is loading for Hall Green on the right but it has come from Bull Street in the left background. The round-ended building behind 3247 was latterly Preedy's the tobacconists but 1880s Victorian photographs show the same building then accommodating Reece Bros who claimed to be 'Ye Oldest Tobacconyst Shop in Bermyngham'! *F W York/ Transport Museum Wythall*

Above: This part of Bull Street (often referred to as Lower Bull Street) retained several small shops prior to total redevelopment on both sides. The Cadbury empire began here. In 1824 John Cadbury opened a shop in Bull Street selling tea, cocoa, chocolate and other goods. From 1831 he rented premises nearby in Crooked Lane, specialising in the manufacture of cocoa products. John's sons, Richard and George, made the world-famous move to Bournville in 1879. Demolition was in progress on 17 June 1968. Although several garages contributed to the Kingstanding - Hall Green services, regular operation of Guys was new, Hockley garage having recently received some 18-year old examples, including 2531. *Malcolm Keeley*

It would be easy to think that Corporation Street was the historic road north out of Birmingham to places such as Lichfield. Corporation Street, however, was a Victorian creation. Dale End can actually claim the honour although today's abbreviated road gives little impression of its former importance. Many bus and tram services used Dale End to approach the city centre, including the 33 from Kingstanding. Perry Barr garage has 1949 Daimler CVD6 1986 on loan in the early 1950s; it was not normally on its allocation. *Transport Museum Wythall*

Masshouse Circus traffic was still not travelling around the full gyratory on 4 November 1968 when BCT 1953 Guy 3022 had the rare company of a Guy with another operator. 888 DUK began life in 1963 as a Guy Arab V demonstrator until sale to Harper Brothers in 1966. Its 72-seat forward-entrance bodywork with distinctive peaked roof was by Strachans. *Malcolm Keeley*

The Gazette Buildings on Corporation Street, near James Watt Street, used to be the home of the Birmingham Gazette, Evening Despatch and Sunday Mercury, still detectable on the stonework in this 1966 picture. These newspapers were sold in the late 1950s to the Birmingham Post & Mail, then based in New Street, near the junction with Corporation Street. The Evening Despatch and Birmingham Mail were great rivals and the 'Spatchy Mail' call of news vendors was familiar across the city centre until the papers were merged. Daimler Fleetline/ Metro-Cammell 3580 is new, the neat dash panel and V-windscreen set the pattern for lower deck fronts until the last Fleetlines were delivered in 1979. *Geoff Kelland/ MRK collection*

The main unloading stop for the Aston Road bus services was here in Whittall Street to the side of the hospital. The tram replacement fleet allocated to Miller Street comprised fifty new Guys and Daimlers, and fifty Crossleys from other garages. 1950 Crossley 2389 was transferred from Washwood Heath garage and remained at Miller Street until the bus was retired in 1967. *S N J White/ The Bus Archive*

This great view of Snow Hill shows the old line of the street down the hill alongside the station. Two buses are working cross-city services, Crossley 2449 leads on the 15 from Hamstead to Yardley followed by a Leyland PD2/Brush on the 29A from Pheasey to Hall Green. Today Midland Metro trams follow the line of this street on grassed track, theoretically giving the trams exclusive access! *Transport Museum Wythall*

Snow Hill Ringway (later Queensway) was built a little further over from the station to feed into the Colmore Circus gyratory. The south side of the Queensway was left undeveloped for many years, allowing photographers good light at any time of the year. BCT was a pioneer of city services without conductors, initially using converted single-door Fleetlines. The 3781-3880 batch of Fleetlines was the first specifically intended for driver only operation, their Park Royal bodies featuring a centre staircase and additional exit. The early examples were allocated to relatively short length inner area services where demolition had thinned demand such as the 69 from Lozells. Fleetline 3785 was only days old when photographed on 21 November 1968. Later examples of the same batch would face a much busier challenge along the Bristol Road. A connection with the last picture is the bus working service 15, in this case Crossley-bodied Daimler CVG6 2787. Snow Hill Queensway is now a canyon among high-rise office blocks. *Malcolm Keeley*

Walsall Corporation Daimler CVG6 889 with Metro-Cammell 72-seat body dating from 1961 is seen more or less in the same position as 2449 but travelling in the opposite direction on the new Colmore Circus. The background never really got sorted out until more recent developments. A BCT MOF Daimler on a 30 to Kingstanding leaves Bull Street. Midland Red's 118 service between Birmingham and Walsall became jointly operated with Walsall Corporation from 8 August 1968. Walsall withdrew most journeys on its service 26 between Walsall town centre and Merrions Close, and removed the protective fare restrictions on the 118. In return Walsall Corporation took a share in the 118, generally using its early 1960s front-entrance AEC Regent Vs and Daimler CVG6s. West Midlands PTE took over Birmingham and Walsall's municipal buses in October 1969 and mopped up the Midland Red share in the 3 December 1973 takeover of the company's West Midlands services. WMPTE extended the 51 from the Scott Arms to Walsall from November 1975 and the 118 disappeared. *Roy Marshall/ The Bus Archive*

MIDLAND RED

ASSOCIATED WITH THE BRITISH ELECTRIC TRACTION CO. LTD. AND BRITISH RAILWAYS

SUNDAY, 4th MAY, 1958
and until further notice

SERVICE No. 118

BIRMINGHAM and WALSALL

Additional Journeys are operated on Mondays to Fridays during Peak hours
and on Saturday afternoons between Six Ways and Walsall

Opposite top: BCT management had great faith in passengers' knowledge of custom and practice; you needed to know that buses displaying CITY were usually short workings of the cross-city 29/29A from Kingstanding and thus the bus would travel via Hockley. 1949 Daimler CVD6/Metro-Cammell 2003 waits alongside the old Snow Hill station for the traffic lights to change. Southbound buses on the once-mighty cross-city services 29/29A were unable to travel directly from Snow Hill to Bull Street after the extended one-way traffic scheme was introduced in August 1936. 2003 will therefore turn left out of Snow Hill into Steelhouse Lane on a long, tedious meander via Lancaster Place and Corporation Street to reach the lower part of Bull Street. *Transport Museum, Wythall*

Opposite: 1951 Daimler CVD6 2656 turns into Summer Lane at the foot of Constitution Hill in September 1968. The background shows the bridge to the north of Snow Hill station constructed over Water Street by the Great Western Railway. In 1954 a newspaper reported that the first buses had been fitted experimentally with the flashing trafficators that were now legal. 2656 was one of those pioneers, being equipped in July of that year. By 1968 2656 was working from Perry Barr garage and had acquired a destination blind intended for an older bus. There was no problem with 'New Look' buses having the older blinds but older buses with 'New Look' blinds were unacceptable as a service number could not be shown. Therefore garages had a few blinds intended for the older buses for emergency use in either generation of bus. *F W York/ Transport Museum Wythall*

Above: Birmingham's first trams, hauled by horses, began running from Snow Hill to Hockley in 1873. The Hockley group of tramways eventually evolved to operate some of BCT's finest electric tramcars running to West Bromwich and beyond, until replaced by buses on 2 April 1939. By then the services arrived at Snow Hill via Livery Street, in those days uninterrupted by the ring road. Passengers were set down here at the Colmore Row end of Livery Street and the vehicles then turned left to load in front of the former Great Western Hotel. The tram replacement routes followed the same loop and were operated jointly with West Bromwich Corporation, including the 74 to Dudley, 75 to Wednesbury and their short workings. BCT introduced Leyland TD6c vehicles like 253 here with 'gearless' torque converter transmission and Metro-Cammell bodies. *Roy Marshall/ The Bus Archive*

Above: The West Bromwich Corporation buses added special interest to these services. West Bromwich recognized that the Birmingham services needed its more powerful buses and almost always allocated those with Gardner 6LW engines. The only regular exceptions were a small batch of Daimler CVD6 buses with Daimler's own engines which were of equal power. One of the latter, no 139, turns the corner in March 1960 with its destination blind slipping badly. It carries a Metro-Cammell body and entered service in 1948. The joint Birmingham and West Bromwich services were not converted to large capacity buses on Mondays to Saturdays until after both operators had been absorbed into West Midlands PTE. *F W York/ Transport Museum Wythall*

Opposite top: The Great Western Railway's Snow Hill station was opened in 1852 and expanded in 1869-71 and 1909-12. The Great Western Hotel was built on the Colmore Row frontage but was not a railway project, despite its name. It ceased to be a hotel in 1906 when the GWR purchased it, providing a passenger entrance through to the station proper, converting the rest of the ground floor to excellent restaurant facilities and the remainder to offices for its own use, much needed due to the expansion of operations. GWR revealed plans in 1939 for a striking replacement building but World War Two and then nationalization meant nothing happened. British Railways concentrated on New Street station in the second half of the 20th century, the former hotel was demolished in 1970 and Snow Hill closed in 1972 until revived by the West Midlands PTE. The Birmingham Post & Mail newspaper group moved from New Street to new premises on Colmore Circus in 1965; the building can be seen under construction in the background. Yardley Wood garage's Brush-bodied Leyland PD2 1696 still has a destination blind dating from its year of construction (1948), its buses would get new blinds upon route changes in November 1964.

Opposite: Across the road from the station on 31 October 1968 is the numeric first of Hockley garage's long-lived 1949 Leylands; new buildings are everywhere and the longer view behind 2131 has become Colmore Circus. 2131 is not working one of Hockley's familiar services. Several garages provided a lunchtime extra or two to give extra capacity between the city centre and the offices at Five Ways. There were several services between the two points so the big question for returning office workers was deciding which shelter or bus stop the lunchtime extras would choose. The 'New Look' buses could show a service number but 2131 here was a lottery! Eventually all the short workings showed service 9. *Malcolm Keeley*

This is the queue outside Snow Hill station on Colmore Row for the Soho Road services through Handsworth, not long after World War Two on 25 March 1949. The shelters are about to be repainted, judging by the ladders. The services were still largely operated by Hockley garage's 1939 tram replacement 'gearless' Leylands. Bus 845, however, was a Metro-Cammell bodied Daimler COG5 with the small Gardner 5LW 7 litre engine, probably one of an injection of extra buses after Hockley garage received further work, and will not be going beyond the city boundary. Hockley garage was about to receive its first post-war buses in the form of 65 powerful new Leyland PD2s. *MRK collection*

BCT introduced all-night bus services on its busier routes in April 1946. They did not use their usual daytime termini, instead they clustered around Bull Street and Colmore Row, near Snow Hill station, so that passengers could interchange from one route to another. To ensure this the Night Inspector every hour would check all the buses had arrived and then blow his Birmingham-made Acme Thunderer whistle, all hell breaking loose as the buses rushed off. The moody 1946 artwork shows the Art Gallery.

Diamond shaped plates on columns marked the beginning and end of roadside reserved for loading buses. On Colmore Row alongside St Philip's Cathedral on 27 June 1966, Crossley 2375 is turning back in the city centre, approximately half the journeys from Perry Common ran across the city as service 7 to Five Ways and Portland Road. Daimler CVG6 1870 is loading for Yardley and Garretts Green Lane. *John Carroll/ Transport Museum Wythall*

After wartime air raid damage to its fleet,.BCT bought 20 unused English Electric bodies from Manchester Corporation. The bodies were available because the new Daimler chassis being built for Manchester were destroyed in the Coventry blitz. One of the bodies was fitted to Daimler COG5 820 and transferred in 1949 to bus 1097, seen loading in Colmore Row. No 1097 was not often photographed and it is even rarer to see a 'Manchester' working the 10 service, the bus being allocated to Quinton garage around 1952-3. *Transport Museum Wythall collection*

Interesting bus stop plates are on view here in Colmore Row, including night service NS62. Loud exhausts pointed directly at the Grand Hotel on the left; guests must have been wakened hourly. The 'New Look' fronts of the buses provide interest. At the rear, Crossley 2516 was a celebrity vehicle, having been exhibited at the Festival of Britain, and was the only Crossley to have a polished flash on the top of its radiator cowl. Daimler introduced the stylized D seen here on Crossley-bodied leading bus 3173 from 2776 onwards. BCT pondered the cost of the chrome strips when 'New Look' grilles needed replacing and the time spent protecting them during repainting. The strips were removed from 24 Crossleys in 1956 including 2516 to see what they looked like - the experiment was not adopted. A later idea from 1960 onwards was to replace grilles beyond repair with the fibre glass creation demonstrated by 3173. *T W Moore*

Opposite top: A short walk along Colmore Row towards Victoria Square and buildings begin again on the eastern side. Possible road widening blighted these buildings so they were not redeveloped. Ironically this saved them, the triangle between Colmore Row, New Street and Bennetts Hill is now a conservation area and the building facades are protected. Colmore Row (then known as Monmouth Street) was redeveloped in the 1870s, becoming the heart of the financial quarter. It benefited on its western side from a continuous line of Italianate palaces with the same cornice level throughout from the Great Western Hotel at Snow Hill station to the Council House. This image was taken on 20 June 1946, just after World War Two, and these two buses still have the camouflage roofs applied by BCT to help disguise buses during air raids. Khaki is Urdu for dusty, a colour adopted by the British Army so troops would blend in with the Indian terrain. It proved so effective at hiding dirt on bus roofs that a shade was adopted for post-war use. Both Metro-Cammell-bodied buses are working useful cross-town services. Leading is 1936 Daimler COG5 844 from Perry Common to Portland Road followed by 'gearless' 1939 Leyland TD6c 246 from Hamstead to Yardley. *MRK collection*

Opposite: Bus 3002 was one of BCT's odd men out, a 1954 one-off lightweight Daimler CLG5 with Metro-Cammell body. An official in 1954 advised the press "We shall give it a fair test and at the end of five years see how it has stood up to constant use and running". Five years was when its initial Certificate of Fitness expired, actually it lasted very well until 1972 when accident damage prompted its retirement. 3002 is loading in 1968 in Victoria Square alongside Christ Church Buildings which replaced Christ Church, demolished in 1899. The replacement became better known as Galloway's Corner, named after the chemist shop opened in the block in 1923. Like many chemists, photographic products were also sold; some of the pictures in this book were taken on a Werra camera purchased from Galloway's. The block was itself demolished in 1970; Victoria Square's open space was then expanded to the proportions familiar today. *John Carroll/ Transport Museum Wythall*

The Council House was built between 1874-9, replacing 18th century buildings on what had previously been called Ann Street. The open area in front of it became Council House Square until renamed Victoria Square in 1901. The driver of Crossley 2326 swings his heavy bus round the tight curve of Galloway's Corner into New Street in 1966. The Bedford van in pursuit belongs to Hawley's, then one of the best known bakeries in Birmingham. *T W Moore*

GOSPEL LANE LOOP 31
VIA SHAFTMOOR LANE

TY·PHOO TEA

JOJ 330

One of the entertainments of the open-back buses was seeing passengers fling themselves off the platforms as they slowed for the turn from Hill Street into Victoria Square. One passenger is ready for his leap into space from Crossley 2330, more volunteers for possible injury will be behind him. The bridge over the road linked the main post office with the sorting office and was demolished in 1974.
T W Moore

Opposite top: 1964 Daimler Fleetline/ Park Royal 3430 enters Victoria Square from Chamberlain Square. The latter square (originally Chamberlain Place) was a picturesque space modelled on an Italian piazza in 1880 to commemorate Rt Hon Joseph Chamberlain's exceptional achievements in Birmingham's politics before moving on to national government in 1876 at the age of 40. Every Brummie will recognize, on the left, the Town Hall opened in 1834. The delightful red brick and terracotta Gothic palace behind 3430, on the doomed western section of Edmund Street, was built in 1885 and originally the Liberal Club. The date is 3 January 1965 and the building would be demolished that year to make way for the new library, part of Paradise Circus. *T W Moore*

Opposite: The Museum & Art Gallery was constructed behind the Council House with its main entrance on Chamberlain Square. It was opened in 1885 by the future King Edward VII, then Prince of Wales. 1950 Crossley 2488 looks splendid in 'as new' condition with the wheel discs originally fitted to 'New Look' (concealed radiator) buses to streamline their appearance. The term 'New Look' originated in 1947 with the voluminous dresses introduced by Paris fashion designer Christian Dior. Brake overheating soon caused concern, however, so firstly the discs were removed and then a gradual programme of shortening front wings began with some buses not being attended to before the grim reaper caught up with them. *Transport Museum Wythall*

Above: The growth of the city meant the administrative centre soon needed extending. A new block along Congreve Street was built in 1910-2 and linked to the original Council House and Art Gallery by a grand arched bridge built over Edmund Street. The new administrative buildings in Congreve Street ran as far as Great Charles Street. Birmingham City Transport occupied many of the offices created in the extension, seen to the right of Daimler CVA6 1554 in Congreve Street in August 1958. Congreve Street was used by Dudley Road and Lodge Road buses heading away from the photographer on their way out of town but there must be a diversion as 1554 is coming the other way, having used the section of Great Charles Street now disappeared under Paradise Circus before turning right into Congreve Street. Buses from Broad Street normally used the similarly disappeared extension of Edmund Street from Easy Row to Chamberlain Square to reach Victoria Square and New Street. Pedestrians are in short supply so it could be a Sunday but it was always a lonely walk for a driver or conductor summoned to Head Office to answer a disciplinary matter. *F W York/ Transport Museum Wythall*

Congreve Street is no longer a road and has become the rather narrower Congreve Passage. The former BCT offices survive; this 1962 view of the other side of Congreve Street from outside the offices looks back towards the Town Hall. This side was completely redeveloped as part of Paradise Circus and has been transformed again in the 2020s. The AEC RT chassis was a superb design to meet the needs of London Transport and BCT received a batch of fifteen in 1947. The collision of BCT and London Transport ideas on body styling put the Park Royal bodies into a class of their own! General Manager A C Baker lived in Moseley on the 1 route and, as 1631-45 were particularly associated with Acocks Green garage which worked the 1, he was able to enjoy these splendid vehicles almost to the office door until his sadly early death in 1950. Mr Baker was replaced by W H Smith who had a Traffic background but in 1962 a new General Manager's name, W G-Copestake, appeared on the sides of the buses. The G with hyphen looked strange; it stood for Goodall and one guesses that its use was to prevent the initials WC! Mr Copestake was previously the Chief Engineer, having his skills in the hot seat was no doubt considered useful as the entire early postwar fleet was falling due for replacement. T W Moore

Midland Red D7 4459, on the same diversion in August 1958, makes the turn from Great Charles Street into Congreve Street. The buildings in the foreground were cleared to make way for Paradise Circus. In the distance we can see buildings on Summer Row that are still with us. Two Leyland PD2s will be turning left into the part of Great Charles Street that still survives, beginning their loop of the City Transport offices. They will then turn right into Margaret Street, certainly impossible since Great Charles Street was widened to dual carriageway. 2175 is one of Hockley garage's Leyland-bodied PD2s working the 96 from Lodge Road while behind is a Park Royal-bodied example, once so familiar working the Dudley Road services. *F W York/ Transport Museum Wythall*

Special occasions closing Victoria Square generated even bigger diversions, the royal visit by HM Queen Elizabeth II in May 1957 causing inbound buses such as Guy 2555 to make this right turn from Great Charles Street into Newhall Street. A small sign directs pedestrians to the Science Museum, then in the other half of Newhall Street and containing preserved BCT tramcar 395. The diverted buses continued down Bennett's Hill to New Street and their normal route. *F W York/ Transport Museum Wythall*

The HAPPY HOLIDAY Way!

DAILY TRIPS AND TOURS
ALL OVER THE MIDLANDS

Official Timetable and Map - Price 3d.
One-day **Anywhere Tickets** - Price 5/-

DAY AND HALF DAY **MOTOR COACH TOURS**
To the Sea and popular Inland Pleasure Resorts. *(See Weekly Bills)*

"**HELPS TO HAPPY HOLIDAYS**" GUIDE, Price 6d.

Complete Itineraries of **COACH CRUISES**, 2, 5, 6, 7 and 12 days. Hotel and Boarding House Directory.

Saloon Buses and Coaches Available for **PRIVATE PARTIES** of every description.

Daily Coach Services by Midland "Red" Associated Motorways and Allied Companies to the popular Seaside Resorts and all parts of the Country.

FOR HOLIDAY TRAVEL ENQUIRIES

Telephone or Call nearest Midland "Red" Office or Agency :

Chief Booking Office	Worcester Street	Mid. 4481
Coach Tour Waiting Room ...	9 Gt. Charles Street	Cent. 7313
Coach Station and Cafe ...	Digbeth	Mid. 4901
Chief Offices	Bearwood	Bearwood 2020

RACE TRIPS
FROM
BIRMINGHAM
(**White Horse Hotel, Great Charles St., near Hall of Memory**)

BEARWOOD, HARBORNE, QUINTON, WARLEY, SUTTON, KINGSTANDING, ERDINGTON, SOLIHULL, OLTON, ACOCKS GREEN, Etc.

PERIOD
1st JAN. to 26th FEB., 1959

SEATS MAY BE BOOKED AT ANY "MIDLAND RED" OFFICE OR AGENCY

No Telephone Bookings will be accepted.

The friendly "Midland Red"

Midland Red's Digbeth Coach Station is very well known and handled the express coach services and the company's high quality extended tours. Less known is that for decades Midland Red's full and half day excursions began from the section of Great Charles Street now lost under Paradise Circus. Business was such that a booking and enquiry office around the corner in Easy Row was opened in 1953, becoming the fourth in the city. The company's numerically first post-war coach, C1 3300 new in 1949, gathers its clients in March 1959 with another C1 and a C3 behind. The excursion coaches transferred to the new Bull Ring Bus Station when it opened in 1963. *F W York/ Transport Museum Wythall*

Above: Some special occasions around Victoria Square caused particularly big diversions, not least the royal visit by HM Queen Elizabeth II in May 1957. Outbound buses to Broad Street normally travelled through Victoria Square into Paradise Street. Crossley-bodied Daimler CVG6 2809 has been diverted onto Great Charles Street. Summer Row is to the left of the photographer and Congreve Street to the right. This became the standard route after Victoria Square was pedestrianised. 2809, however, is about to enter the part of Great Charles Street that, as previously noted, disappeared into Paradise Circus. *F W York/ Transport Museum Wythall*

Opposite top: The Dudley Road services were jointly operated by Birmingham City Transport and Midland Red. The latter had so many routes that its purely local services in some towns and cities had an appropriate letter prefix and two numbers. The Dudley Road services were numbered B80 to B89, the B for Birmingham prefixes being carried by BCT buses too. The setting-down point for passengers heading into the city centre was here in Margaret Street. BCT's buses were supplied by Rosebery Street and an inspector from that garage was often positioned here to sort out any timekeeping issues. They seemed more genial than most inspectors, perhaps because they avoided the wrath of the waiting passengers in Edmund Street. 50 Park Royal-bodied Leyland PD2s, 2181-2230, were delivered in 1949-50. Park Royal employed its standard shell design with its splendid, powerful, front profile while incorporating as many BCT features as possible. The lower numbered examples spent most of their lives working from Hockley garage, the remainder at Rosebery Street. 2181-95 lacked the characteristic swoop in the blue band below their front destination boxes. In 1968 2217 is working the B80 while 2181 is on driver tuition and is parked by the back entrance to BCT's offices. Driver tuition buses were a useful extra resource to get a package quickly from a garage to Head Office! *John Carroll/ Transport Museum Wythall*

Opposite: Edmund Street, graced by the grand arched bridge between the original Council House and Art Gallery and the block containing the BCT offices, was the loading point for the Dudley Road group of services before and after the conversion of trams. BCT's pre-war fleet was entirely replaced by 1955 so the reinstatement of some Daimler COG5 buses in 1957-8 was a delightful Indian summer for these buses. They were apparently allocated where destination blinds existed for them, 814 being returned to service at Rosebery Street garage. 814 had been damaged in a wartime air raid and rebodied with an unused English Electric body intended for Manchester Corporation. It is turning into Congreve Street en route for Soho in March 1959. *F W York/ Transport Museum Wythall*

The 1880s enlargement of New Street station saw the incorporation of Great Queen Street and destruction of the old street pattern. Station Street was created on its southern boundary and from 1922 would become a most important terminus for Midland Red services. It was handy for shopping and markets yet was a relatively quiet backwater. Station Street was then a much longer road, stretching from John Bright Street to Worcester Street, at the western end of the Market Hall. The latter section beyond Dudley Street was lost under the construction of the Bull Ring Shopping Centre, built between 1961 and 1964. This March 1957 view of 1948 S8 3265 and 1955 S14 4300 looks along the vanished section towards the Market Hall. *F W York/ Transport Museum Wythall*

Midland Red D5B 3801 loads at the Market Hall end of Station Street where the company provided a line of cast iron passenger shelters, as can be seen gracing them with the term 'Bus Station'. The Market Hall was behind the photographer; the dilapidated buildings on the left of the picture lined part of Worcester Street. Appropriate as 3801 was headed for Worcester and would take 2 hours 20 minutes to reach its ultimate terminus in the Malverns. 3801 entered service at the beginning of 1951 and looks almost new here. *R T Wilson*

Above: Allenways was an important coach operator with a departure stand in Station Street where this Foden is loading passengers looking forward to the races. Allenways head office was then in Balsall Heath, close to BCT's Moseley Road depot, before its move to Fortnum Close, Tile Cross. Allenways was sold to the owner of Claribel Coaches in 1986 and use of the name ceased in 1992. The "Crellin-Duplex" patent design of half-decker coach was first produced by Lincolnshire Trailers, building 11 such coaches before ceasing trading. The patent was then picked up by Mann Egerton, building 9 more by 1953. Allenways purchased two in 1950 on Foden chassis, itself a relatively rare choice. KOC 662-3 were given the names "City of Birmingham" and "City of Lincoln" by Allenways. The design could carry around ten more passengers than a standard coach of similar dimensions and these Fodens seated 43. Seats were arranged in groups of four, the pairs facing each other. Most people disliked facing strangers and around half, of course, had to travel backwards. Those in the lower compartments suffered poor visibility and felt claustrophobic – hardly the "Pullman" experience claimed. *Transport Museum Wythall collection*

Opposite: Midland Red's Station Street services mostly served to the west. BCT meanwhile offered a choice of city termini to its passengers along the Coventry and Stratford Roads in the south-east of Birmingham. The Station Street routes served the markets area while alternatives went via the Bull Ring to the High Street area and primarily met shoppers' demands. The Coventry Road tram services were replaced by trolleybuses from January 1934, the Stratford Road trams by motorbuses three years later. The trolleybuses were ousted by motorbuses in July 1951. The markets routes to the Coventry and Stratford Roads were gradually withdrawn as passengers voted with their feet for the Bull Ring/ High Street area. The 57B to Yardley was withdrawn in March 1961. Bus 2630, one of the Daimler CVD6 buses delivered in 1951 to replace the trolleybuses, is ready to move into Dudley Street in May 1959. Daimler CVD6 1783 stands behind at the 28 terminus which remained in this area for many years, lacking a High Street alternative. *F W York/ Transport Museum Wythall*

Above: The Repertory Theatre, opened in 1913, fronted onto Station Street and had a worldwide reputation. It moved to its new theatre on Broad Street in 1971 but the Station Street premises are still in use as the Old Rep. Hinckley Street, seen here at the back of the Repertory Theatre, is a great survivor of the 20th century demolitions. In October 1957 the 28 has been diverted into Hinckley Street and a stop column planted. The pedestrians behind Daimler CVD6 2097 are walking along Dudley Street and beyond them in the background is Old Meeting Street, a narrow road leading to the Market Hall. 2097 has a blind intended for an earlier design of bus, note the space created when the 28A was renumbered 28 and the A painted out. *F W York/ Transport Museum Wythall*

Opposite top: Among buildings demolished for the Victorian expansion of New Street station was the Old Meeting House. Memory of the latter lived on with the survival of Old Meeting Street where Midland Red 1951 S12 3770 had been left pending its next work in March 1959. The Market Hall is behind the photographer who can just see the back of the Repertory Theatre to his right but his view of the extensive work creating Smallbrook Ringway is largely hidden by the bus and the shambolic fencing. It is interesting to see the first section of the five storey Ringway offices and shops under construction over the entry point to Hurst Street, identifiable by its raked columns. Old Meeting Street was removed from the map by the Bull Ring Shopping Centre. *F W York/Transport Museum Wythall*

Opposite: Prior to the construction of the Bull Ring Bus Station, Midland Red maintained various premises around the Station Street area in addition to the Passenger Enquiry & Booking Office around the corner at no 27 Worcester Street. A yard included a gravity-feed refueling facility until December 1953. Parcels were handled from this office at no 54 Dudley Street. Behind the unobtrusive shop front were offices at the back and above. The parcels business had its origins in the BET's "Tramways Parcels Express", from 1905 conveying parcels via its tramway systems. Vans later took over the heavier goods until the latter business was transferred to Pickfords but lighter parcels continued to be sent by Midland Red service buses until 1980. Eventually there were around 550 parcels receiving offices and agencies handling more than a quarter of a million packages annually. Parcels boys with handcarts or bicycles were familiar across the city centre, in this picture a Midland Red parcels bike is dwarfed by BCT Daimler CVD6 2067 in March 1957. Hinckley Street junction is behind the photographer. *F W York/ Transport Museum Wythall*

Move on to February 1959
and Dudley Street is looking
rather different as the
buildings behind 2067 in
the last picture have gone
and Bryant's construction
huts are prominent. Midland
Red's parcels business is
in temporary premises in
Pershore Street until the
new bus station opens.
Behind Daimler CVG6 1610
is a good view of New Street
Station's roof, patched
up after severe damage in
World War Two. To the left,
the back of the Repertory
Theatre marks the beginning
of Hinckley Street. *F W York/
Transport Museum Wythall*

Walk a little further along
Dudley Street and, from
the mid-1950s, the
construction works for
Smallbrook Ringway would
be inescapable. Daimler
CVD6 1952 is moving from
Dudley Street into Pershore
Street. It is crossing the
former junction with
Edgbaston Street (on the
right), Smallbrook Street and
Worcester Street, cleared
for the Ringway by the time
of this March 1958 view.
The Daimler's manouevre is
still possible today as the
Ringway, now Queensway,
is raised on an intrusive
overbridge. Behind 1952
can be seen the whole
length of Hinckley Street.
*F W York/ Transport Museum
Wythall*

The end result of the massive construction is seen in December 1968 with Smallbrook Ringway on its raised alignment hidden by the Bull Ring Centre. Walsall Corporation 1961 72-seat Willowbrook-bodied AEC Regent V 899 has just left Midland Red's bus station at the end of Edgbaston Street and is only a few feet away from where Daimler 1952 was photographed. Walsall Corporation first obtained a licence to operate into Birmingham city centre in June 1965, its service 158 from Bloxwich to Union Street usually employing the operator's recently delivered Northern Counties-bodied Fleetlines. The 118, however, generally received slightly older front-entrance Daimler CVG6s or Regent Vs like 899. *John Carroll/ Transport Museum Wythall*

The new Bull Ring Centre included Midland Red's fully undercover bus station which was opened by the Lord Mayor of Birmingham in November 1963. The Bull Ring Bus Station brought all the company's Birmingham services into one central terminus for the first time (except the Dudley Road group jointly operated with Birmingham City Transport out of Edmund Street and long-distance services which continued to use Digbeth Coach Station). This was obviously a great improvement over the previously widely scattered street termini in the old Bull Ring, Station Street, New Street, Navigation Street and Paradise Street that had been so unsatisfactory for those changing from one route to another. Midland Red's main passenger booking and enquiry office moved into the West Mall of the new Bull Ring Centre where there was a restaurant and cafeteria. Buses entered the Bus Station via Dudley Street, leaving via Edgbaston Street. Inside were 29 departure stands, a staff canteen and offices for inspectors, parcels and left luggage. All good in principle but sadly it quickly became a fume-filled damp cavern. After Midland Red's division, successor operators gradually moved out leading to closure. *David Barber collection*

Originally traffic from the Bull Ring direction could turn right from the Ringway into Hill Street. This was later considered dangerous, the gap was closed and the traffic had to make a full circuit of Holloway Circus which itself was tedious to enter. Among bus routes so afflicted was the 17; the driver of 1952 Crossley-bodied Daimler CVG6 2801 is blocking other traffic so that 2785's driver, making a hand signal, gets precedence on 30 August 1968.
Malcolm Keeley

This is the major traffic junction replaced by Holloway Circus. Behind the photographer is Horse Fair, leading to Bristol Street. Leading off to the left is Holloway Head. A surprisingly narrow Suffolk Street is visible and John Bright Street is behind the bus. Smallbrook Street is on the right. 1947 Daimler CVG6 1572 in February 1957 is heading for Holloway Head, and will then travel via Five Ways and Harborne to reach Weoley Castle. *F W York/ Transport Museum Wythall*

This is John Bright Street near the start of Station Street in the fine summer of July 1959 with a fine collection of BCT ironmongery on the pavement. 1948 Leyland PD2/ Brush 1699 works the cross-town 34 between Kingstanding and Quinton via Holloway Head, numbered 33 in the opposite direction. Previously two separate services on opposite sides of the city, the 33/34 were linked in 1930 when it was the policy of the Transport Committee to help reduce traffic congestion by minimising the number of bus services making the full circuit of the city centre. Good idea provided the two sides remained evenly balanced. Massive new housing estates were soon constructed in Kingstanding while the Holloway Head route to Quinton remained relatively unsuccessful and became an infrequent peaks only extension. Other cross-town services became similarly afflicted, although to a lesser extent, and needed extra journeys on one side of the city. *F W York/ Transport Museum Wythall*

The large building in the background was the Central Technical College in Suffolk Street, opened in 1895. Latterly known as Matthew Boulton Technical College, it was demolished in the late 1960s. One of BCT's celebrity vehicles makes the turn from Navigation Street into John Bright Street. In July 1956 2926 reappeared after collision repairs with the straight staircase replaced by a steeper one, permitting the total number of seats to increase by two to 57 and causing the loss of the small window at the offside rear of the lower deck. 2926 was also re-equipped throughout with Auster double deflector ventilators; the rainwater moulding above the upper deck windows was also removed. *Transport Museum Wythall*

Leyland PD2/ Park Royal 2218 occupies the same space as 2926 but we are looking up Hill Street towards Victoria Square on 11 May 1958. The right turn from Navigation Street to John Bright Street must have been a worrying manoeuvre to those driving up Hill Street and unfamiliar with the arrangement. *John Carroll/ Transport Museum Wythall*

1950 'New Look' Crossley 2438 in Hill Street is clearly very new and its perfect appearance contrasts with the once splendid roof of New Street station, critically damaged in World War Two. Tram wires and rails remain although the last services using them, to Moseley and King's Heath, had been replaced by buses the previous year. They survived as part of the access route for Bristol Road and Pershore Road tramcars from Selly Oak and Cotteridge depots requiring Kyotts Lake Road tram works in Sparkbrook. *S J Butler*

An atmospheric view of Hill Street is dominated by Daimler CVD6 2016 in February 1959. Navigation Street runs across the middle background. Hill Street's short, sharp gradient up to Victoria Square is in the distance with a BCT bus making the climb. A Midland Red S15 with black roof loads at the bottom of the incline. The photographer was always keen to record buses loaned to his local garage, Moseley Road, while its own CVD6s were being overhauled upon Certificates of Fitness expiry. 2016 was then normally resident at Acocks Green. *F W York/ Transport Museum Wythall*

Some Midland Red Hagley Road services were terminated at the Queen's Hotel end of Navigation Street to relieve overcrowded Station Street. This interesting visitor is one of six AEC Regents with Brush bodies built to the order of City of Coventry Transport but diverted when new in 1942 to Midland Red. The bodies of the six Regents were extensively rebuilt in 1951 and looked quite different afterwards. *R A Mills/ MRK collection*

The Stephenson Street end of Navigation Street was dominated by the huge bulk of the Queen's Hotel. On the right in July 1961, Gene Kelly and Donald O'Connor impersonators try to impress a favourite conductress while practising for the Midland Red Annual Dinner and Dance! The passengers of D7 4082 await the end of the performance while the driver of BCT Crossley-bodied Daimler CVG6 3210 can only envy both their energy and the layover time enjoyed by Midland Red crews in the centre of town – BCT crews had to keep moving!. *Malcolm Keeley*

Opposite top: Midland Red 5192 entering Navigation Street was one of a hundred LS18 class Leyland Leopards built in 1962-3. Twenty, including 5192, when new were finished to dual-purpose 'black roof' specification. 5192 was new to Sutton Coldfield garage and, glamour days over, was still working from there on the 113, a 37-minute run from the Hardwick Arms, Streetly. D9 5328 follows, its journey on the 110 from Tamworth almost completed. 5192 was transferred to Stratford garage in 1971 and thus did not pass to the West Midlands PTE under the 1973 deal. *Malcolm Keeley*

Opposite: The continuing increase in Midland Red activities after World War Two caused the terminus of the services to Blackheath, Wolverhampton Road and Sandon Road to be transferred to Paradise Street. Queen's College Chambers on Paradise Street was built in 1904 and, fortunately, its terracotta façade was retained during redevelopment in the 1970s. It is visible to the rear of one of Midland Red's rarer wartime intake. 2440 was a Leyland TD7, one of three with Northern Counties bodies allocated to the company by the Ministry of War Transport in 1942 and run until 1955. *S N J White/ The Bus Archive*

Above: A gloomy April 1959 view along the full length of Paradise Street; Christ Church Buildings on Victoria Square provides the atmospheric backdrop beyond the Town Hall. This is another Daimler CVD6 loaned to Moseley Road garage while its own were being overhauled upon Certificates of Fitness expiry. CVD6 1802 was normally a resident of Hockley garage, behind it Midland Red D5 3512 and a D7 wait for their departure times. The introduction of MoT tests was a death blow to many old cars like this Austin. *F W York/ Transport Museum Wythall*

Above: 1959 was a very good summer but this day in August was clearly an exception. Through the murk you can see how the building line of Broad Street on the right hand side of the picture had been changed in anticipation of road widening to come. Those changes certainly came and the same scene today is packed with important buildings including Symphony Hall, the Birmingham Repertory Theatre, The Library of Birmingham and the Hyatt Regency. A few older buildings survive such as Baskerville House, the Hall of Memory and the former headquarters of the Birmingham Municipal Bank, all now looking tiny! Back in 1959, the bus is another Midland Red rarity, no 3575 being one of the 20-strong GD6 class dating from 1949. These were Guy Arab III models whose original Meadows 6DC engines were soon replaced by BMMO 8 litre units. The bodies were also built by Guy, using Park Royal frames. The twenty were particularly associated with Dudley garage and scrapped around 1962. *F W York/ Transport Museum Wythall*

Opposite top: The City Council in the 1960s and 1970s developed Broad Street as a business area and a series of high rise blocks, both commercial and residential, was constructed at Five Ways. The area was being transformed at the time of this 19 July 1968 picture looking back along Broad Street. The sun reflects off a tall office block where the huge gyratory and underpass was still to come. Metro-Cammell bodied Fleetlines 3391-3400 introduced BCT to new styles of windscreens, the six with flat v-screens set the standard for BCT and WMPTE Fleetlines until the end of their long production run in 1979. 3399-3400 additionally had experimental Clayton Dewandre 'Compas' heating and ventilation systems, allowing the number of ventilators to be reduced. This lucky shot shows curved screen 3400 being pursued by flat screen 3399 on service 3 to Ridgacre Lane. *Malcolm Keeley*

Opposite: Work on the underpass at Five Ways had begun by the date of this 23 January 1969 picture with temporary bridges over the excavations. Two-door Fleetline/Park Royal 3786 has come from Islington Row which is flanked by the two office blocks in the background. 3786 is entering what had been Ladywood Road, then in the process of becoming Ladywood Middleway. *Malcolm Keeley*

Old Birmingham is giving way to the new in this view of Bath Row and 1950 Leyland PD2/ Park Royal 2222 on 1 June 1968. On the right, one can see right across the city centre to the new GPO tower. The large new block on the left is Cumberland House at 200 Broad Street where the West Midland Traffic Commissioner was situated for many years. Many a bus company employee wearily entered Cumberland House with applications for service revisions, if necessary ready to do battle with objectors. *Paul Gray/ Transport Museum Wythall*

There has been total change here since the 1950s. Bristol Street is now a multi-lane dual carriageway and traffic is encouraged to avoid the city centre by using the broad Middleway, the crossing of the two highways grade separated by an underpass. Back in 1952 traffic avoiding the centre had to use historic streets; at least this crossing had been blessed with traffic lights. Working along Bristol Street is 826, one of the last standard tramcars to be received. The batch of thirty, 812-41 delivered in 1928-9, were particularly associated with Cotteridge depot and the Pershore Road service. Pershore Road trams accessed Bristol Street via Pebble Mill Road and Bristol Road while the replacing buses would use Belgrave Road. *Peter Mitchell*

The City Circle was launched in March 1932 and was the closest of BCT's three circulars to the city centre. 1949 Daimler CVG6/ Metro-Cammell no 1916 battles its way through the congested inner areas in March 1959, turning from Bristol Street into Benacre Street. *F W York/ Transport Museum Wythall*

The City Circle was never the runaway success of the already introduced Inner and Outer Circles but it was a useful facility before the widespread demolitions along its route. The City Circle in parts, however, was sometimes so close to the Inner Circle that the passengers could almost wave to each other, damaging the potential of the former. Crossley 2446 climbs Great Colmore Street, Lee Bank in April 1957 and would be turning right into Cregoe Street. Much of this housing was in poor condition and was soon swept away by comprehensive redevelopment. *F W York/ Transport Museum Wythall*

Had 2446 continued a little further along Great Colmore Street it would have met the Inner Circle at this point. The thoroughfare with the downward gradient on the left is Great Colmore Street. Leyland PD2 2180 is exiting Lee Bank Road to cross Wheeley's Road and enter Islington Row in October 1957. BCT had its own design of moquette produced by Lister's to adorn the lower saloons of its standard buses. The non-standard nature of the Leyland bodies on 2131-80 extended to the seat design and the pattern of upholstery. *F W York/ Transport Museum Wythall*

The transformation of Lee Bank and other inner areas meant the old streets disappeared and the Inner Circle was often transferred to the new middle ring road to be called the Middleway. Work on the new road was incomplete on 11 May 1968. Liverpool Street garage has received its first allocation of Guys eighteen years after they entered service! The soft springs of 2572 have caught this driver out as he moves from the old Lee Bank alignment to the new, just west of Bristol Road. *Malcolm Keeley*

Passengers' eye view as Daimler CVG6 2784 is expertly photographed at Summer Hill from earlier CVG6 no 1923 on 3 October 1968. The scene is eerily reminiscent of the early days of the Berlin Wall where buildings along the border were initially bricked up. *Monty Russell/ Transport Museum Wythall*

The driver of Crossley 2517 tackles another knotty set of City Circle streets as he moves from Powell Street across Camden Street on his way into Albion Street in April 1957. *F W York/ Transport Museum Wythall*

The 96 bus route that replaced the notoriously twisting and hilly 32 tram service to Winson Green was one of two chosen by BCT to test the strengths of the first two British designs of rear-engine double-deck buses. Birmingham's very first rear-engine bus was this Leyland demonstrator, a 1960 Metro-Cammell bodied Atlantean initially worked on service 14. It was purchased with effect from 1 May 1961 and numbered 3230. The punishing regime on the 14 proved to BCT that the rear-engine concept was satisfactory and it ordered ten Atlanteans and ten Daimler Fleetlines for extended trials. 3230 had a brief period at Rosebery Street garage until it was transferred to Hockley for the 96 in July 1961. 3230 is descending Newhall Hill in the Jewellery Quarter, then still very Dickensian. *Geoff Kelland/ MRK collection*

Photographs 1946-1969: Around the Suburbs

Only just outside the city centre, this is where the Inner Circle bus route crosses the Dudley Road group of services. Guy 2538 waits in Icknield Street for the traffic lights to change while PD2/ Park Royal 2228 on the B82 moves from Spring Hill into Summer Hill Road on 15 April 1968. The Inner Circle route here nowadays follows part of the Middleway but somehow Spring Hill Library, built 1891-3, has managed to dodge demolition despite being in direct line of route and is now Grade II listed. *Paul Gray/ Transport Museum Wythall*

Midland Red allocated a large number of new FEDDs to Oldbury garage as its share of the Dudley Road tramway replacements in 1939. Many of these FEDDs worked hard for very many years on the 'Track', as the route was nicknamed. 1939 FEDD 2374 (FHA 878), with rebuilt Brush 56-seat body, is making yet another journey along the Dudley Road, near Bellefield Road, in July of the hot summer of 1959. *F W York/ Transport Museum Wythall*

Opposite top: Most of the Park Royal-bodied PD2s worked from Rosebery Street garage until its closure in 1968, largely working the Dudley Road services operated jointly with Midland Red. 2215 stays inside Birmingham on 1 June 1968 by working B80 shorts to Grove Lane, on the boundary with Smethwick, a 12 minute run barely two miles from the city centre. The best seats in the Grove Cinema were in the circle and then cost 4 shillings and 6 pence (22.5p). *Paul Gray/ Transport Museum Wythall*

Opposite: The B82 continued across the boundary through Smethwick to Bearwood, terminating in the bus station after its opening. The driver of the BCT Leyland PD2 working the B82 inserts his key in the Bundy timekeeping clock. The 220 and 221 services via different routes to West Bromwich were jointly operated by Midland Red and West Bromwich Corporation. BCT regarded its wartime Daimlers as sub-standard and sold them early. West Bromwich, however, prolonged theirs - in many cases by rebuilding the deteriorating austerity bodies or rebodying them with either new or transferred bodies from older vehicles. One of the lucky ones was CWA6 127 which looks a brand new bus, having received this Alexander 56-seat body in 1953. Alexander was an unusual choice for an English operator in those days. *Gordon Davies*

Above: Midland Red 1950 S10 3666 ran its entire 15-year life from Oldbury garage where there were few opportunities for the crews to enjoy rural rides. A call to operate this journey on the X82 to Kinver (an extension on leisure days of the frequent 130 to Stourbridge) in March 1959 was therefore a treat. 3666 passes the King's Head, on the opposite corner to Bearwood Bus Station which the Birmingham via Hagley Road services did not enter. *F W York/ Transport Museum Wythall*

Opposite top: The exotic 1320-3 were Daimler COG6 buses with Metro-Cammell bodies delivered in 1941-2, originally intended for South Africa and not shipped due to World War Two. They were eight feet wide, six inches wider than permitted in the UK under normal circumstances in those days. They were not originally allowed in the city centre and allocated to Yardley Wood for the inter-suburban 18 service between Haunch Lane and the further reaches of Northfield. Postwar width relaxation allowed them to be reallocated to service 9 between the city centre and Quinton. No 1322 is inbound and well-laden on the Hagley Road, just the city side of the King's Head in 1949. Behind is Midland Red's first S9, 3357, spending its first few months working from Bearwood garage, a contributor to the 130 Stourbridge - Birmingham service which had been converted to double-deckers the previous year with brand new AD2s! WMPTE extended the 9 to Stourbridge in November 1983, replacing the 130. *S J Butler collection*

Opposite: It is a challenge for any major urban highway to retain its tree-lined splendour; at the time of writing the Hagley Road through Edgbaston has survived reasonably well. The enigmatic destination CITY was more associated with short workings of the 29/29A Kingstanding – Hall Green services. Here Perry Barr garage's Crossley 2386 is displaying it on the Hagley Road, could passengers wanting Broad Street find themselves following the 33 down Holloway Head instead? Presumably the regulars knew where 2386 was going, it was well laden and being energetically driven on 22 June 1967. *Paul Gray/ Transport Museum Wythall*

Above: Birmingham was the first UK city to introduce one-man operated double-deck buses on ordinary services. This began on 11 June 1967 when three routes were converted to one-man operation on Sundays only, including the 6 to Sandon Road. Suitably modified Fleetline/ Metro-Cammell 3546 was seen on Sandon Road on that first Sunday. The first seven day a week conversion followed on 16 July with service 96 to Winson Green. *Paul Gray/ Transport Museum Wythall*

One of the most attractive suburbs in Birmingham is Harborne and 1954 Guy 3068 looks suitably smart on Croftdown Road on 8 September 1969. Continuing housing development to the west of the city periodically caused demand for further bus services, even in wartime when the 10 was introduced on 19 May 1940. The need for more bus accommodation in the area was already evident and land at Quinton was identified in 1939 for a garage to house 150 vehicles. It finally opened on 30 October 1949 for only 100 buses under cover, relieving Harborne garage including taking over the 10 route. *Paul Gray/ Transport Museum Wythall*

The London and North Western Railway arrived in Harborne in 1874 which changed from a country village to a thriving suburb by the turn of the century and absorbed into Birmingham in 1891. Inbound trains frequently suffered long delays entering the main line to New Street so bus competition made easy inroads into passenger carryings. The Harborne horse bus route was one of the first converted to motorbuses by BMMO. Rail passenger services ended as early as November 1934 although the line remained open for goods trains for another three decades. Crossley 2503 on Harborne Road crosses from Edgbaston into Harborne in July 1966. *F W York/ Transport Museum Wythall*

The growth of Queen Elizabeth Hospital has meant much of Vincent Drive is now surrounded by buildings. There is a new link road into the hospital and, in contrast, this end of Vincent Drive is now reduced to a pedestrian path. The trees have been allowed to grow and the idea of it ever being a bus route seems remote. This is Crossley 2494 on inter-suburban route 2 from the Ivy Bush heading for King's Heath in the 1960s. In the distance, beyond the prominent old chimney, is the tall campanile clock tower of Birmingham University which moved out of the city centre to its new site off Bristol Road, Bourn Brook, in the early years of the 20th century. *R Mallabon/ Transport Museum Wythall*

This view of the important bus stop in Chapel Lane, Selly Oak shows the depot in the background. For many years Selly Oak depot ran both tramcars and buses but in 1951, to create space for the imminent tram conversion, all double-deck bus work was transferred to other garages, particularly Harborne. Materials were still in short supply and blind linen was expensive so the Selly Oak blinds were transferred to certain exposed radiator buses at Harborne to work the 20 group. Nearly all these were Daimlers but there were exposed radiator Crossleys on Harborne's strength, including 2307 here in June 1957. As the rest of Harborne's allocation did not have the 20 group destinations on their blinds, including all the 'New Look' buses, they were rarely seen on Weoley Castle until major service changes in July 1957. Then the 20 group was renumbered 21 and 22, by which time shortages had been overcome and all Harborne's buses could receive new blinds. *F W York/ Transport Museum Wythall*

Above: Weoley Park Road, Lodge Hill, pleasingly retains much of the same feel today as in this November 1957 view although, of course, traffic has increased. Gibbins Road is to the left and Shenley Fields Road to the right. 1947 Daimler CVA6 1552 on the recently introduced 21 service has the roads to itself. *F W York/ Transport Museum Wythall*

Opposite top: Mist, mature trees and backlighting in Shenley Fields Road combine in this moody, split-second view of 1950 Guy 2531 on 10 October 1969. The bus looks pure BCT but has been owned by WMPTE for ten days; new fleetnames will obscure the Birmingham coats-of-arms any day now. The BCT buses were well specified and maintained. With inadequate deliveries of new buses in the early1970s, WMPTE engineers were obliged to offer some BCT 'Standards' for short-term extensions of their Certificates of Fitness and were sometimes surprised to get longer tickets than expected. *Paul Gray/ Transport Museum Wythall*

Opposite: In Weoley Castle, many shops were built around Castle Square - to be pedantic not exactly square but a large traffic island about to be entered by recently delivered Fleetline/Park Royal 3871 on Beckbury Road on 15 October 1969. Considering the battering to trade local shops have endured in recent years, Castle Square today continues to look busy. *Paul Gray/ Transport Museum Wythall*

The magnificent passenger shelter constructed at Rednal terminus around the tram turning circle was a famous part of the tramway system and needed on fine days. Buses took over in July 1952 by which time other attractions were becoming available. This view of Crossley 2287 shows just the beginning of the passenger shelter, not surprisingly few passengers were around on 1 March 1959. *Barry Ware*

While the Rednal turning circle had been turned into 'a pleasance, with grass plots, shrubs, footpaths and seats', Rubery terminus was never as grand but still attractive. This was the setting-down stop in August 1962, buses picked up on the other side of the A38. Crossleys 2284 and 2276 were both newly overhauled. The Bristol Road services would be BCT's first large-scale driver only conversion, commencing on the day man landed on the moon, Sunday 20 July 1969. The public had been softened up with a short period of double crew pay-as-you-enter operation and, with the assistance of an excellent printed pamphlet handed out in generous numbers in Navigation Street, they cottoned on well. *John Carroll/ Transport Museum Wythall*

Birmingham can be proud of its leafy suburban roads. 1948 Brush-bodied Leyland PD2 1708 with its exceptionally shiny chrome radiator surround climbs Church Road, Northfield on 31 May 1968, providing a short working of the 18 as far as Northfield centre. *Malcolm Keeley*

Northfield's Church Road in those days flowed smoothly into Bunbury Road, seen here. Yardley Wood garage added BCT's trial Atlanteans to its already large collection of Leylands in 1967. 3238 with Metro-Cammell body and dating from 1961 was also snapped on 31 May 1968 on the same short working but was able to show the 18D route identification. *Malcolm Keeley*

Above: The principal activities of Birmingham's single-deck buses were services in the southwest of the city, operating under the low railway bridges near Bournville and Northfield stations. The 27 from Kings Heath notably served Cadbury's works and the Bournville Estate beyond, developed by that inspired family for its workers as a model for housing estates. Most of Birmingham's early post-war fleet of single-deck buses were 1950 Leyland Tiger PS2 buses bodied by Metro-Cammell's partner company, Weymann. The height obstruction at Bournville Lane, where 2252 is emerging, also involved a canal alongside the railway. Bournville Station is located here and, in honour of Cadburys, is nowadays painted purple. 2252 was later the first PS2 conversion to driver only, the alterations being completed in February 1966. *R Mallabon/ Transport Museum Wythall*

Opposite top: Such peace as Scottie the dog ambles slowly across the empty roadway. But at certain times of the day there is absolute mayhem here when some of the most popular people in the world start or leave work at the factory behind the photographer. This is Bournville Lane, home of Cadbury's chocolate, and on 20 March 1969 Leyland PS2 2246 waits at the loading stop for West Heath. 2246 is on a Northfield short working and is probably the first of many extras that will gather and clear the crowds at factory leaving time. The 27 timetable had to accommodate an earlier Friday finish, not to forget the 'Special Friday' variation when every fourth week workers went home at lunchtime, causing single-deckers and their crews to be dragged out for just one trip. The 27 had a relatively early evening peak, one single-decker finishing in sufficient time to rush into 'Town' and make a worthwhile contribution to the main Bristol Road services. *Malcolm Keeley*

Opposite bottom: The Pershore Road remains very narrow through Stirchley and inbound vehicles of all kinds use Hazelwell Street in the city-bound direction, rejoining Pershore Road at the junction with Umberslade Road. Co-operative societies have been merging for many years but, back in 1953, the Ten Acres & Stirchley Co-operative Society (shortened to TASCOS) was still going strong and its centrepiece premises can be seen behind 1947 Daimler CVG6 1558, loading at a 'dolly' (temporary) stop. The store is decorated for the Coronation of HM Queen Elizabeth II; BCT's contribution to the celebrations is the fitting of two small Union flags beneath the destination box. The TASCOS site is dominated today by a store of one of the national supermarket chains. Early post-war materials shortages were still being felt, 1558's semaphore trafficators are not fitted in front of the first lower deck window and the space is covered by a small panel. Some new buses did not receive them, additionally they were prone to damage and replacements could not always be obtained. Many of the early post-war buses ran for years without them, some probably never receiving them before flashing indicators were legalized and retrofitted in the late 1950s. The 36 tram service had terminated in the centre of Cotteridge but the replacing 45 bus service, introduced in 1952, was extended to West Heath. This simplified travel for West Heath residents who previously had to catch another bus, the 23 group, to reach Cotteridge and change there to the tram service. Some buses continued to provide shorter journeys, like 1558 here which had commenced its journey at Kings Norton Green. These 'shorts' were used to create a branch route, numbered 41, to serve new housing in Turves Green from 1957. *S N J White/ The Bus Archive*

Opposite top: The order for Leyland single-deckers delivered in 1950 was modified to include five of the new underfloor-engine Leyland Olympic model which were of the rarer 27 feet 6 inches variation. These were very suitable when the first driver only buses in Birmingham for over 30 years were introduced from 1 December 1963 on a new service 4, linking the new Pool Farm estate with the important shopping area of Cotteridge where passengers could catch citybound and Outer Circle buses. 2261 is seen on Walkers Heath Road on 20 May 1967, the background hinting of its recent rural past. *Paul Gray/ Transport Museum Wythall*

Opposite bottom: The single-deckers were assisted by a crew-operated double-decker on weekday evenings. Like the Leyland Olympics, 1953 Crossley-bodied Daimler CVG6 2892 was provided by Yardley Wood garage and was seen at the Cotteridge terminus on 20 March 1969. *Malcolm Keeley*

Above: Balsall Heath with its poor quality housing has changed out of all recognition since this picture was taken in the mid-60s. 1951 Daimler CVD6 2105 is on a 48 short working from the city centre to King's Heath and is leaving Cox Street West to enter Lincoln Street, passing Clevedon Road on the left and Upper Cox Street on the right. Buses could use the narrow streets in both directions but, in earlier days, this would have been the single track route taken by trams <u>into</u> the city centre, the outbound trams having to use adjacent streets. *R Mallabon/ Transport Museum Wythall*

Opposite top: King's Heath was an early thriving residential suburb. Its railway station opened in 1840 (as the original Moseley station) but, like elsewhere in the city as its boundaries expanded, its suburban trains fell victim to the good frequencies and cheaper fares offered by the Corporation's trams and buses. All the stations on the Camp Hill line were closed to passengers in January 1941 as a wartime economy and not reopened. In due course, buses claimed all the public transport market in King's Heath, replacing the trams in 1949. 1937 Daimler COG5 1060 is on a short working in September 1958, nearing the end of its journey in King's Heath's High Street. *F W York/ Transport Museum Wythall*

Opposite: The first sections of the Outer Circle were introduced in January 1923, the route being finally created on 7 April 1926 by the linking of two services, including the 11, the number retained for the new circular. Many parts of the route were still rural in character so riding all the way round became a day out, rivalling the tram ride to the Lickeys. The Outer Circle made the greatest impact ever by buses in Birmingham and the Tramway Committee reported "In all probability future transport developments in the city …. will lie with this system of transport". The single-deckers in use were immediately overwhelmed. The answer was BCT's latest AEC 504 double-deck buses which had introduced top covers and proved the reliability and flexibility of the motorbus. All Saints' Church in King's Heath is the backdrop in September 1958 as veteran Daimler COG5 953, first licensed in January 1937, turns right from Vicarage Road for a brief sashay along Alcester Road before turning left into Addison Road. *F W York/ Transport Museum Wythall*

Above: The Outer Circle continues to thrive and still follows most of the roads used on its introduction, a fascinating mix of old lanes, sometimes barely improved in width but elsewhere upgraded to dual carriageway. The route was nicknamed 'The Desert' by the crews because there is no terminus, buses pressing on endlessly! In BCT days the round journey of 24.8 miles took 130 minutes, reduced to 120 on Sundays. There were three timing points in each direction, policed by Bundy timekeeping clocks, two of which were also smoking points to give crews a brief release from the pressure. Awkward crossings of radial main roads and unexpected delays such as road works ate away at any spare time. Crossley 2504 makes slow progress along Vicarage Road in October 1967. *F W York/ Transport Museum Wythall*

Above: Demand varied considerably around the Outer Circle with schools in particular generating surges of passengers. These were handled by short workings such as this one in Vicarage Road, setting down at a handsome lollipop-shape stop and travelling as far as Hagley Road in July 1957. The use of a single-deck bus in the form of Leyland PS2 2233 is exceptional, however. *F W York/ Transport Museum Wythall*

Opposite top: BCT developed an interesting selection of inter-suburban services radiating from King's Heath. All Saints Road was a useful turning opportunity and terminus for them. From 1949 buses from the city centre on King's Heath short workings also used All Saints Road as a terminus loop although these lessened as housing developments continued further out. In recent years local residents have understandably pulled up the proverbial drawbridge on buses. 1947 Daimler CVA6 1537 works the 2B in July 1957 linking King's Heath with Selly Park and Bournbrook, the Queen Elizabeth Hospital and the Ivy Bush on Hagley Road. *F W York/ Transport Museum Wythall*

Opposite: The service number 35 along the Moseley Road and Alcester Road has a long and interesting history. The number was reused for a new driver only service commenced on 31 October 1965 to link Brandwood estate with the existing bus network at King's Heath. It became yet another route terminating in All Saints Road, seen here on an unpleasant slushy day although 1965 Daimler Fleetline/ Marshall single-decker 3470 managed to remain shiny! The 35 joined the ranks of city radial services from 18 May 1975 when it was linked to the 49 City - Leopold Street – King's Heath route, at the same time being extended further outwards to Pool Farm. *Maurice Collignon*

The 35's approach to Brandwood Park Road was via Allen's Croft Road where this unusual visitor was seen. FXE 892C was a Bedford VAM with Strachans 46-seat body. Unusually it was a demonstrator for the body rather than the chassis builder and was loaned to BCT for no less than three months in 1965-6, running from Selly Oak, Moseley Road and Yardley Wood garages. No business resulted for Bedford but Strachans was rewarded with the body contract for Fords 3651-62. *R Mallabon/ Transport Museum Wythall*

By the 1950s it was impossible to find a BCT bus in a country location but one could find occasional hints of the rural past. The inter-suburban 18 route was introduced in 1929 and followed the then southern extremities of Birmingham's housing developments. Crossley-bodied Daimler CVG6 2861 is seen on Monyhull Hall Road in March 1959. *F W York/ Transport Museum Wythall*

This is the slightly oddly named area known as Alcester Lanes End. Brush-bodied Leyland 1677 on inter-suburban service 18 from Haunch Lane queues in Taylor Road on the approach to Alcester Road on 16 October 1965. 1677's grille has been refreshed with a coat of black paint and contrasts well against the dark blue bonnet.
Monty Russell/ Transport Museum Wythall

Moseley is an ancient settlement and was already a thriving suburb connected to central Birmingham by railway and tram when it was absorbed into the city in 1911. St Mary's Church existed by 1496, a new structure was built in 1780 and rebuilt somewhat since. Moseley Village saw some development in the 1870s but changed little through the 20th century; 1947 Daimler CVG6 1580 passes through during July 1959, a glorious summer. This class of Daimler was not normally operated by Acocks Green garage which ran the 1A.
F W York/ Transport Museum Wythall

Above: The strange overgrown building in the background is now demolished but was on the corner of College Road and Wake Green Road in Moseley. It appears on old photographs as the entrance to Moseley Botanical Gardens and the Pine Dell Hydropathic Establishment. These opened in 1892 and closed as early as 1900. Pine Dell's facilities were housed in the former Spring Hill College, built in 1854-7. The college buildings in 1923 became Moseley Secondary School, later Moseley Grammar. In post-comprehensive days it is now simply Moseley School. Miraculously, at some expense over the years, the school's impressive 'Birmingham Gothic' buildings have survived. Crossley 2337 has stormed College Road hill and has a clear run into Wake Green Road in July 1959; today's drivers encounter white lines and a pesky raised mini-roundabout. *F W York/ Transport Museum Wythall*

Opposite above: It took an hour to travel the 10.6 miles around the Inner Circle. There was a Bundy timekeeping clock and smoking point at Saltley and two other timekeeping clocks in each direction to ensure crews did not run early. One Bundy clock in the anticlockwise direction was at Highgate Road where 2880 is seen waiting on 14 July 1962. Each driver had a key for the Bundy clock. Every key had a different number, thus identifying the driver. When he inserted and turned the key, it recorded the unique number and the time on a paper tape inside for an inspector to check. Passengers thought drivers loved the clocks so much that each one was happy to wind them up at every opportunity; the truth was rather different! Two Birmingham Crossley-bodied Daimler CVG6s received these fibreglass bonnet cowls, a later design introduced by Daimler, 2799 being the other. 2880 was allocated to Highgate Road garage, just visible behind the bus on the opposite side of the road. This was 2880's last day there as the garage was closed that evening. Highgate Road's work on the Inner Circle was added to Liverpool Street's share. 2880, however, moved to Yardley Wood with the 37 route. *Monty Russell/ Transport Museum Wythall*

The 36 service was introduced in 1936 as a rather oddly shaped radial service commencing in the city centre from Station Street. It travelled along Stratford Road through Sparkbrook, branching off at Formans Road to serve the Tyseley factory area and terminated in Stechford. In 1958 the city end was withdrawn and the 36 became an inter-suburban service using varying Sparkbrook streets over the years to turn in the vicinity of the junction of Stratford Road and Stoney Lane where it connected with the Inner Circle 8. Highgate Road garage basically ran the 36 until its closure in 1962 when responsibility passed to Acocks Green. Other garages, however, helped to clear the factory demands. In March 1959 Highgate Road's Crossley-bodied Daimler CVG6 2873 awaits departure time in Mole Street, two of Yardley Wood's Brush-bodied Leylands are also loitering on positioning journeys. The fire damage to St Agatha's Church roof was due to a vandal, considered very shocking at the time. *F W York/ Transport Museum Wythall*

On Stratford Road in October 1958, bus 1486 passes the junction with Mole Street while working the cross-city 29A service from Pheasey Estate to the Baldwin, Hall Green. 1486 belonged to Birmingham's first batch of 75 post-war 'Standard' buses delivered in 1947. These were Daimler CVA6 buses with AEC 7.7 engines, continuing the type of engine fitted to the wartime Daimlers. By 1950 BCT had received 425 exposed radiator Daimlers with Metro-Cammell bodies, the rest having Gardner 6LW or Daimler's own CD6 engines. Only one of these 425 Daimlers exists today, CVA6 1486 at Wythall. *F W York/ Transport Museum Wythall*

When BCT introduced its grand changeover to electric trams on New Year's Day 1907, a branch off the Stratford Road service was opened along Stoney Lane as far as Doris Road, then on the fringes of the city until the 1911 boundary extensions. Birmingham belonged to Warwickshire until 1974 and its pre-1911 boundary is on the horizon of this picture taken at the junction of Stoney Lane and Showell Green Lane in August 1957. Up to 1911 Moseley lay entirely in Worcestershire although divided between two councils. The bulk of Moseley off-camera to the left was part of King's Norton while this spot near Wake Green was within Yardley Rural District. The Yardley Wood Road services were divided through Sparkbrook and Sparkhill after the Stratford Road trams were withdrawn in 1937. The 13/13A travelled via Stoney Lane to replace the withdrawn tramway while the 24 continued to use Showell Green Lane. Bus 296 is of exceptional interest, being a prototype Leyland PD2 built in 1947 and a grandfather of the thousands of PD2 and PD3 Titans sold worldwide. It had a body also by Leyland that did not conform to BCT standards; despite this the bus ran until 1967. In the left background a Daimler approaches along Stoney Lane on the 13. *F W York/ Transport Museum Wythall*

A bus terminus was created at the junction of Yardley Wood Road and Haunch Lane, better known as 'The Valley', a dip hollowed out by Chinn Brook. Initially used by service 13, it became the eastern terminus of the important inter-suburban 18 to Northfield and beyond. The Leyland PD2/ Brush in the background has just travelled down the hill from nearby Yardley Wood garage and is pulling off Yardley Wood Road into the 18 terminus bay. Part of BCT's small single-deck fleet was employed on Education Department contracts involving children with special needs which may explain Leyland PS2/ Weymann 2258 loitering in Haunch Lane on 12 September 1967. The increasing requirement for 'one-man' single-deckers in the 1960s was partly met by retaining many of the ageing 1950 Leyland PS2 buses with Weymann 34-seat bodies that the single-deck Fleetlines should have replaced. The cabs of several were suitably modified so that the driver could collect the fares, although not particularly comfortably. *Paul Gray/ Transport Museum Wythall*

The 29A (later 90/91) route was fascinating after it turned off the Stratford Road to serve the parts of Hall Green beyond easy walk of the main road tramway. Bus drivers had to know where they were going as the route weaved along old and new roads to the Baldwin terminus. Sarehole Road was one of the new roads constructed, being employed by Crossley 2398 in May 1967. Sarehole was a separate hamlet where the young J R R Tolkien lived between 1896 and 1900, before the area was overwhelmed by Birmingham. He described Sarehole as 'a kind of lost paradise' and its mill made a deep impression on him. One wonders what Tolkien thought of the road outside the mill becoming a timing and smoking point for Outer Circle bus crews! Sarehole ceased to be a working mill in 1919 but happily it has been restored as a museum. Another celebrity resided nearby in his earliest years, comedian Tony Hancock lived in Southam Road. *Paul Gray/ Transport Museum Wythall*

Opposite top: Even before Hall Green began to be developed, Brook Lane, Robin Hood Lane and Webb Lane were realigned so that they met and required only one bridge under the North Warwickshire railway line, opened in 1908 and the last to be built in the Birmingham area. Leyland PD2/ Park Royal 2192 is seen on Robin Hood Lane on 21 September 1967, the opportunity to widen this section to dual carriageway has never been taken. 2192 has passed under the height restricted bridge which certain buses are still not allowed to encounter today. The fencing marks the line of Robin Hood Crescent which provides the link from the bridge to the historic alignment of Robin Hood Lane. Off the picture to the left is Webb Lane, which managed both to retain a rural character and have a vehicle factory, for years accommodating battery-electric manufacturer Electricars. It is unlikely that the photographer then thought he would become a leading light in the preservation of battery-electric vehicles at Wythall. *Paul Gray/ Transport Museum Wythall*

Opposite: This excellent view of Kedleston Road, Hall Green, taken on 21 September 1967, shows its curves and the dip that buses used to charge down as fast as possible to reduce the need for gear changes on the upward side! The buses were narrower then and private cars fewer so the roars of Leylands like Brush-bodied 1738 were rarely interrupted. The Ford Thames van parked in the dip is taking a chance, though! *Paul Gray/ Transport Museum Wythall*

Above: Bad weather besets the crew of Leyland-bodied Leyland 2176 on 9 January 1968. The bus is turning from Scriber's Lane into Baldwin's Lane; the blinds have already been turned from 91 Hall Green to 90 for its return journey. Leyland was able to supply 50 bodies at a very good price on half of the 100 Leyland PD2 chassis ordered to become BCT's 2131-2230 and delivered in 1949-50. The Leyland bodies on 2131-80, however, were to the manufacturer's standard design apart from swivelling windows in the drivers' cabs and the layout of the half-drop ventilators. Angled staircases permitted a capacity of 56 seats, compared to 54 on buses with the Birmingham straight staircase. *Malcolm Keeley*

Above: The same location but viewed from the opposite direction. The bus has just started from Baldwin's Lane terminus and is turning into Scriber's Lane with its generous supply of trees now in leaf. The season promises better weather but Leyland/ Park Royal 2191 and the photographer have both received a thorough drenching and the gutters are full of water on 27 May 1968. *Paul Gray/ Transport Museum Wythall*

Opposite top: The River Cole restricted further tramway progress along the Stratford Road until a new bridge enabled an extension in 1914 to the Bull's Head at Fox Hollies Road and the development of that part of Hall Green. Midland Red 1944 Daimler CWA6/ Duple 2533, in unrebuilt condition, has just crossed the bridge on its way to the city centre in September 1948, passing the site of a steam tram depot long since closed behind the photographer. In the background is the College Arms, built at the time of the new bridge and in the nostalgic half-timbered style so typical of public houses of that period, and two Birmingham Daimler COG5s. The 154 ran from Solihull via Shirley and is a direct predecessor of today's 6 service. *S J Butler (G H F Atkins collection)*

Opposite: The gradient from the River Cole is known as Green Bank and, after construction of the new bridge started, shops began to be provided at the top. The gabled examples behind the bus were built in 1913 and bear the legend Hall Green Parade. An unexpected and delightful move in March 1968 was the transfer of some of these 1949 Leyland PD2/ Park Royal buses to Yardley Wood garage, 2195 being seen on 27 May. *Paul Gray/ Transport Museum Wythall*

THE BIRMINGHAM AND MIDLAND MOTOR
OMNIBUS COMPANY LIMITED

NOTICE TO PASSENGERS

REDUCTIONS IN FARES

On 31st DECEMBER, 1957, the Company announced that certain fares up to the level of 4d. would be reduced by $\frac{1}{2}$d. and the reductions would be introduced as soon as new Fare Books had been printed.

This formidable task is now completed and the reduced fares will become effective as from SATURDAY, 1st MARCH, 1958.

It will assist the Conductor if all passengers will state the journey being made.

Information as to any particular fare can be obtained as from 1st March, either from any of the Company's Offices or from the Fare Books carried by all Conductors.

Chief Traffic Offices:
BEARWOOD.
February, 1958

D. M. SINCLAIR, General Manager

Above: One of the last tramway extensions was the Stratford Road line, further extended in April 1928 on central reservation to the city boundary with Shirley in Solihull Rural District to serve Hall Green's massive planned housing. Buses took over in January 1937. Shirley was then the preserve of Midland Red under the 1914 agreement so BCT buses turned at the city boundary through a gap in the broad grassed central reservation. 9 January 1968 was a dreadful day for snowfall. Leyland PD2/Brush 1688 had probably lost at least one round journey and the driver was making only the briefest of pauses at Hall Green terminus. Gritters had made no impact by mid-morning, the main road was as bad as the bus terminus. Tough drivers and conductors could earn extra money in the depths of winter shovelling a salt mixture off a small fleet of Daimler COG5 buses converted to lorries to help keep the bus routes open. "Lovely job" said one conductor, literally through gritted teeth. *Malcolm Keeley*

Opposite top: Stratford Blue buses, from 1952 sharing Midland Red's 150 route to Stratford-upon-Avon, have been seen earlier in this book. Stratford Blue initially used its latest PD2s but by the turn of the '60s they had been transferred to other services and older JUE batch open-platform PD2s were usual. 1950 Leyland PS2s whose single-deck bodies had been replaced with new double-deck bodies by Northern Counties followed in 1963 until Stratford Blue's increasing fleet of PD3s took over. No 4 was built in 1963 with Willowbrook bodywork and belonged to the first batch with concealed radiators, it is seen at the city boundary on 6 September 1969. Stratford Blue's three Leyland Atlanteans also worked on the 150 from late 1967. Stratford Blue and its 116 staff were fully absorbed by Midland Red on 1 January 1971. *Malcolm Keeley*

Opposite: Gospel Lane was known as Beeches Lane until the 1920s. Part of its length formed the city boundary with Olton, in Solihull, and included the terminus of the busy Gospel Lane loop bus services. Bus crews took their balancing time here, passengers riding around the loop could change to the previous bus if it was still on the stop. When Solihull introduced new houses on its side of Gospel Lane, on the site behind AEC RT-type Regent 1638, the Birmingham councillors were free to remain deaf to the complaints of the new Olton residents suffering from Corporation buses ticking over outside their homes and blocking their drives! *G H Stone*

Above: The Warwick Road tramway was replaced at the same time as the Stratford Road. The replacement 44 bus service introduced in January 1937 extended the service from the centre of Acocks Green to the boundary with Olton, turning at the junction with Olton Boulevard East. The 44 was then extended in April 1939 as service 44A via Lincoln Road and Lincoln Road North to terminate at Clay Lane, turning at the junction with The Vineries. This fine picture shows two buses on the 44A working through Greet in May 1959, 1937 Daimler COG5 1024 being 'pushed' by Guy 2576. *F W York/ Transport Museum Wythall*

Opposite top: Acocks Green was within the boundaries of Yardley Rural District Council but the railway station on Sherbourne Road meant the suburban lifestyle was well established before Birmingham's 1911 takeover. Midland Red competed with the trains with services linking the city centre through Acocks Green to Solihull and beyond. The company also began from 1938 a cluster of local services from the centre of Acocks Green to Olton and then fanning out to Wythall, Yardley and later to Sheldon. 1950 BMMO S12 3737 is working one of these suburban locals and, having loaded up, is now on its way, beginning with an almost total circuit of the traffic island in the village centre. *Ken Jubb*

Opposite: The Coventry Road trolleybuses may have been able to ignore the disused tram tracks still in place here on Kingston Hill, looking towards the Birmingham City FC ground, but their overhead could be intrusive. Bordesley Park Road strikes off to the right, taking with it the 28 bus route and before that the 22 tram. The only vehicle on the move is Leyland trolleybus 34, almost silent. How peaceful – today this is a major traffic island on the Middleway ring road. At the top of the hill is a Midland Red bus and another trolleybus outside Arthur Street (Coventry Road) depot. A significant reason for raising bus fares in the 1950s was the eye-watering increases in fuel tax. Retaining electric traction probably wouldn't have escaped the many rising costs either, in particular nationalisation of the electricity supply ended beneficial municipal rates. Residents around the Coventry Road liked their quiet trolleybuses and still talked about them decades after they were gone. *R T Wilson*

This is Coventry Road near Green Lane junction in August 1969. It was then a lively local shopping centre; nearest the camera is Glarry's fashion shop 'where only the look is expensive'. Crossley-bodied Daimler CVG6 3167 travels out of town towards Yardley. Sometimes it would be even livelier here as St Andrew's, the home of Birmingham City Football Club, is just around the corner behind the bus. *F W York/ Transport Museum Wythall*

The village of Hay Mills, where the Coventry Road crosses the River Cole, became a suburb as development continued beyond Small Heath towards Yardley. BCT placed just one order for standee single-deckers, 18 AEC Swifts with Metro-Cammell bodies, numbered 3663-80 and delivered in 1967. They were initially allocated to Acocks Green garage for service 36 (Stechford – Sparkbrook) which had heavy peak requirements to the factories in Tyseley and light off-peak demand. For the transport operator, the route thus had all the right attributes for standee buses but the passengers loathed them and in May 1969 they were reallocated to Selly Oak for service 27 which had to have single-deckers. The 36 briefly ran along the Coventry Road in Hay Mills while crossing between Kings Road and Berkeley Road. 3666 and 3674 pass each other in October 1967 on the Coventry Road, long before the road was widened. *F W York/ Transport Museum Wythall*

Above: The old Yardley belonged in Worcestershire, its incorporation into Birmingham in 1911 caused a change of county to Warwickshire. The Coventry Road trams and the replacing trolleybuses terminated here in South Yardley at the 'Swan' where the Outer Circle bus route crossed after its introduction. The 'Swan' tramway terminus was unusual on the Birmingham system in having a turning circle, the only other one being at Rednal. Replacement trolleybuses from 1934 turning at the 'Swan' continued to use the same circle as did the motorbuses that took over in 1951 until the Coventry Road was massively widened in the 1960s to include an underpass for through traffic. Sheldon was added to the city in 1931 and quickly began to be developed, the trolleybus wires being extended in July 1936. The peak vehicle requirement in the busy early post-war years was no less than 56 trolleybuses on the Albert Street services and 8 on the Station Street - Yardley route. The number of trolleybuses available was 74, this is Leyland 18 at the 'Swan' shortly before the conversion to buses. The 'Swan' is off-camera on the left. Once an attractive country inn, by 1967 it had become a massive new public house with several bars, a level of facilities that proved unsustainable. Apartments now occupy the site. *R T Wilson*

Opposite top: Sheldon belonged to Meriden Rural District Council before 1931. Midland Red provided facilities to the area which were reduced as Birmingham City Transport introduced its services. Some Midland Red services remained including the 175, linking Marston Green through Sheldon to Solihull and Shirley. 4295 loads in Church Road, Sheldon Heath in May 1957. This section of road was served only by Midland Red but, being within Birmingham, BCT has provided the stop column. The company's Digbeth garage did not have many S14s, 4295 being a rare exception. All these earlier S14s originally assumed the provision of conductors although many were later modified as driver only operation spread. *F W York/ Transport Museum Wythall*

Opposite: The Yew Tree was briefly the terminus for the Hob Moor Road 15 service but it was soon extended outwards as Yardley developed, eventually as far as Whittington Oval in 1949. Buses were linked from 1929 to Handsworth Wood and, later, Hamstead, showing service 16 in this direction. Leyland-bodied PD2 2140 with highly polished radiator passes prefabricated houses in Queens Road, Yardley, on 21 September 1967. The prefabs were built as an emergency measure after World War Two but they were very popular, being better specified than many of the houses residents previously occupied.
Paul Gray/ Transport Museum Wythall

As housing developments in the Yardley area extended, a variation of the 15/16 service was introduced in 1938. This was the 15B, commencing in the city centre and branching off at the Yew Tree to Garretts Green island (Garretts Green Lane/ Sheldon Heath Road). Daimler CVG6/ Metro-Cammell 1895 is seen at the terminus with Crossley 2447 behind on 25 February 1953. The destination is not a romantic gesture from the driver to his favourite conductress; the bus will be turning just short of the city centre loop. The 15B was extended from 1958 along Garretts Green Lane to the Meadway and renumbered 17.
R A Mills

This spot, at the junction of Bordesley Green East and Stuarts Road, for many years was BCT's terminus in Stechford. It marked the end of a broad dual carriageway whose central reservation was originally the tramway; in August 1928 the last reserved track route extension to be completed. Planned conversion to buses in 1940 was delayed by World War Two and its aftermath but achieved in October 1948. BCT converted the Stechford services to Daimler Fleetlines in February 1969 when 3293 with Park Royal body was seen with Midland Red Alexander-bodied Fleetline 5254; both buses were new in 1963. The 53 route recently had been progressively extended to Tile Cross Road following road improvements along Meadway; 3293 is on a short working to the old terminus. The construction of the huge Chelmsley Wood estate, just beyond the Birmingham boundary, began in 1967 and the 163 via Bordesley Green, Meadway and East Meadway was Midland Red's first service. Variations to serve different parts of Chelmsley Wood soon followed. *Maurice Collignon*

Above: A well-laden football extra supplied by Perry Barr garage assists service 53 on Bordesley Green East, passing the end of Levante Gardens on 30 March 1968. Coventry Road garage with its fleet of Daimlers operated the usual vehicles on the 53/54 so Brush-bodied Leyland PD2 1701 was quite a contrast; similar 1721 can be seen in the background about to cross Station Road and the Outer Circle. Crews were instructed to avoid the dreaded 'SERVICE EXTRA' if a suitable appropriate destination was available. The main football grounds appeared on all destination blinds but it was inevitable that 1701 and 1721 with their Perry Barr blinds would have to show 'SERVICE EXTRA' when travelling in the opposite direction along this corridor. *Paul Gray/ Transport Museum Wythall*

Opposite top: Fancy that, someone has taken the P out of M & B's Export beer! Crossley 2392 began and finished its life working from Washwood Heath garage. It is bound for the city centre and is turning left, having passed under the railway overbridge in Saltley Road. When new in 1950 it would have turned into Great Francis Street. Duddeston and Nechells, however, was the first of the comprehensive redevelopment areas to be approved. A much modified street pattern means 2392 is entering a new alignment, Melvina Road, into an area that had changed utterly by the date of the photograph, 12 June 1967. *Paul Gray/ Transport Museum Wythall*

Opposite: Looking in the opposite direction into Melvina Road, the lady reclining on the railway embankment is not the goddess of gricers. The statue is called 'Youth', sculpted by Harry Seager and formally unveiled in 1959. The date is May 1967 and the 55 service, almost entirely in the care of Washwood Heath garage, basically had been operated with Fleetlines since 1963. Odd journeys were still scheduled for rear-entrance buses including this working from Lea Hall garage employing 1949 Daimler CVG6 1882. *Paul Gray/ Transport Museum Wythall*

The Capitol cinema, near the railway bridge on Alum Rock Road, on 22 April 1963 was showing a film starring Edward G Robinson. He had a long career and was one of Hollywood's most intelligent actors, although largely remembered today for his gangster roles in the 1930s. Passing by is Daimler CVG6 1601 which also had a long career of nearly 19 years, lasting well into 1966.
Monty Russell/ Transport Museum Wythall

Opposite top: The approaches on either side of the crossing over the River Cole at Stechford have long been a nightmare. Traffic both on the outer ring road and between the city centre and Tile Cross share the bridge on Station Road. 1949 Daimler CVG6 1892 was providing vintage transportation for Tile Cross passengers on 18 July 1968, the 14 by then normally Fleetlines. 1892 was approaching the stop shared with the 11 Outer Circle outside the Bull's Head public house, also now history. The River Cole is today bridged by a dual carriageway. *Malcolm Keeley*

Opposite bottom: The depot in Washwood Heath Road opened for tramcars in January 1907. It also operated the Nechells trolleybuses from 1922 to 1940 while motorbuses ran from there from time to time. This included taking a share in the 14 service from August 1946, receiving a collection of pre-war and wartime Daimlers from Liverpool Street. Ten Daimlers are lined up in Washwood Heath's yard; CWA6 models 1414 (Park Royal body), 1430 and 1426 (Duple), a COG5, two more CWA6s (one Park Royal from the 1385-92 batch and a 1359-65 batch Duple) and finally four more COG5s. The new Lea Hall garage took over the 14 to Tile Cross from Liverpool Street and Washwood Heath in April 1955. The major arrival of motorbuses came on 1 October 1950 when the depot's tramcars working the Alum Rock and Washwood Heath services were replaced. The new 55 and 56 motorbus services were extended beyond the tram termini to Shard End (in stages) and Castle Bromwich respectively. *A Yates*

Above: Arguably the ultimate picture of Birmingham City Transport buses, this huge gathering is clearing demand from the Birmingham Race Course at Bromford Bridge on Easter Monday 29 March 1948. The queue of buses pointing west on Bromford Lane is led by 1939 Daimler COG5 1230 and one of the four 1945 Brush austerity-bodied Daimler CWA6 vehicles, 1471-4. Many more buses are lined up among the houses in the background. There is barely a private car or post-war bus to be seen. The racecourse is now the site of Bromford Bridge estate. BCT introduced the 26 to serve the new estate on 11 September 1967. The 26 was then a feeder to the existing radial services, terminating at the junction of Alum Rock Road and Highfield Road. Its first buses were 1950 Leyland-MCW Olympic single-deckers converted to driver only, replaced by double-deck Daimler Fleetlines from May 1968. *Transport Museum Wythall collection*

The Cuckoo Road terminus in Nechells during July 1952 and the dreariness of the old housing is plain to see. Not much of interest for cuckoos here although the compulsory stop plate is rather choice. This was the original trolleybus route, numbered 7, suspended and replaced by buses in 1940 during World War Two with the electric vehicles never returning. 1949 Daimler CVD6 1958 waits for its crew to 'peg' the Bundy clock and commence the journey of around 13 minutes to the city centre. *Transport Museum Wythall*

The Nechells service, worked by Liverpool Street garage, became the second test route for rear-engine buses. Leyland Atlanteans 3231-40 arrived first and were initially placed into service at Hockley on service 96. As soon as trial Fleetlines 3241-50 arrived, the two batches were distributed equally between Hockley and Liverpool Street. Here Atlantean 3237 tackles a tight corner in Nechells. Daimler won the trials and no more Atlanteans were ordered. The Atlanteans were concentrated at Hockley and the ten prototype Fleetlines at Liverpool Street from May 1964. 16 trolleybuses had been purchased in 1932 for the Nechells service including maintenance spares. The extra seats and declining passenger numbers in the inner area meant that only five large capacity buses proved necessary for the 43, plus a maintenance spare. For the time being the remainder were scattered on other work from Liverpool Street until the ten prototype Fleetlines were exchanged in the autumn of 1964 with Perry Barr for production Fleetlines 3251-6 and four Daimler CVD6s. *R Mallabon/ Transport Museum Wythall*

Interesting domestic architecture was to be found on the Inner Circle, including this wedge-shaped building in Nechells Place in October 1967. In BCT days, short workings of the circular services did not show a service number. Daimler CVD6 2704 has BCT's own design of cheap grille, usually fitted in the 1960s after collision damage. *F W York/ Transport Museum Wythall*

A service numbered 8 between Saltley, Small Heath and Sparkbrook began in February 1926 and extended via Five Ways to Hockley in August. It was finally extended in February 1928 via Aston to Saltley to form the complete Inner Circle. This busy view of Inner Circle buses was taken on Rocky Lane, Aston in October 1967. 1949 Daimler CVG6 1920 is heading towards Nechells Green. *F W York/ Transport Museum Wythall*

From 1912 there was a two-way circular tram service between the city centre and Witton Square, in one direction via Six Ways, Aston and New Town Row and, in the other, via Park Road (later largely wiped out by the Aston Expressway) and Aston Cross. The portion via New Town Row fell victim to service cuts at the beginning of World War Two but the Aston Cross half continued until replaced from 1 January 1950 by the 39 bus. 1947 Daimler CVA6 1541 is well on its way back to the city centre, being seen at the junction of Aston Road and New John Street in August 1959. The main Aston Road services (64-67) were operated by Miller Street garage, local to this spot, and the buses in the background are awaiting changes of crews. Miller Street used to have a foundry where the Bundy timekeeping clocks and iron bases of tramway standards were cast. The foundry also manufactured lamp posts for the city's Gas Department and manholes and drain covers for the Public Works Department. *F W York/ Transport Museum Wythall*

The crew enjoy some momentary relief on the anticlockwise direction of 'The Desert' (Outer Circle) at the Stockland Green Bundy timekeeping clock. Crossley 2323 of Acocks Green garage waits alongside what little remains of the green; its driver must be stretching his legs and is not to be seen. Drivers had to explain on a Running Report any irregularity of 1 minute or more early, or 3 minutes or more late at a Bundy clock. Two familiar abbreviations were CVT for congestion of vehicle traffic and HPT for heavy passenger traffic. *Geoff Kelland/ MRK collection*

Witton Square was also served from 1926 by the Perry Common bus service and the Outer Circle which still share Brookvale Road as far as The Ridgeway. Leyland PD2 1715 travels past the Witton Arms on an Outer Circle short working on 20 April 1968, as usual in those days not carrying a route number. Brush chose to display a body for Birmingham at the 1948 Commercial Motor Show. Its Show line-up already included a single-deck body on Leyland chassis. Brush had a tilt test problem with this contract and felt Leyland had been unhelpful in solving it. Perhaps for one or both of those reasons, Brush modified the body intended for 1715 to fit one of Birmingham's Daimler CVD6 chassis and displayed that combination. The CVD6 in due course entered service carrying its intended Metro-Cammell body as bus 1843. *Paul Gray/ Transport Museum Wythall*

Opposite: The Sacred Heart and St Margaret Mary Roman Catholic Church provides a dramatic backdrop to Perry Common service 5 short workings led by 1947 Daimler CVG6 1571 in Witton Road, Aston during October 1958. BCT made considerable use of short workings. It carried around one and a quarter million passengers every weekday around this period, most of them seemingly travelling between 0700 to 0900, and 1600 to 1800. Some short workings were positioning or garage journeys but others enabled the buses to have sufficient time to make another constructive journey, each time saving a bus and crew. *F W York/ Transport Museum Wythall*

Above: The Inner Circle still travels west from Aston Cross via Park Lane towards Newtown. 1948 Daimler CVG6 1874 is on Park Lane approaching its then junction with High Street, Aston. Park Lane lacked the appeal of its well-known London namesake and represents the streets Inner Circle drivers had to endure; needless to say the traffic arrangements here are very different today. *Geoff Kelland/ MRK collection*

Below: It seemed no building was safe in the 1960s so we can be grateful that the splendid late Victorian Barton's Arms in Aston has survived. On 16 May 1967 the widening of High Street, Aston to dual carriageway is taking place and Harper Brothers ex-London Transport RTL-class Leyland OLD 820 rolls with the temporary corners. It is working a peak limited stop journey; Harpers drivers had the reputation of not hanging about, this one no doubt employing all the RTL's plentiful power to keep on time. *Paul Gray/ Transport Museum Wythall*

Have you got a light mac? Plenty to keep you dry here on Great Hampton Street in Hockley as 1949 Leyland PD2/ Brush 1740 passes the Swallow Raincoats factory on 19 September 1967. The Barclays Bank in the background is on the corner of Great King Street. *Paul Gray/ Transport Museum Wythall*

The depot in Whitmore Street, Hockley began life in 1888 with the cable trams, replaced in due course by overhead electric trams. The April 1939 tram to bus conversion was greatly assisted by a building extension allowing many of the replacing buses to be parked in readiness while the trams remained in operation. This extra space then allowed the Dudley Road replacement buses to be worked from Hockley throughout World War Two until their natural home, Rosebery Street depot, could be made available in 1947. This was not without hazard as Hockley depot and its contents were severely damaged in a wartime air raid in October 1940. The spare space also allowed Hockley to extend its activities. Participation in the Inner Circle and cross-town services meant Hockley's distinctive Leylands became widely seen across the city. BCT had several generations of ticket vans built on former motorbus chassis. The last vans were built by Riverlee in 1947 on 1935 Daimler COG5 chassis. Most were retired around the time of the conversion from traditional Bell Punch equipment to 'Ultimate' ticket machines which took place between 1950 and 1954. AOG 679, however, lived on as the 'bank van', taking all the small change collected on the buses to the bank, guarded by a cluster of conductors. It awaits its next cargo of copper, silver and multi-sided threepenny bits on the forecourt of Hockley garage on a dank day around late 1960. *Transport Museum Wythall collection*

Heathfield Road may not have pointed towards 'Town' but it was busy with those bus routes from Perry Barr and Kingstanding that, instead of travelling directly via Aston, side-stepped across to serve Hockley and its factories. The 69, however, began in Lozells and thus was commencing its journey to the city centre. Here in 1950 is a rare nearside view of a Birmingham 1939 Leyland TD6c; no 291 with Metro-Cammell body is followed by a post-war Leyland PD2/ Brush. *Transport Museum Wythall*

Leyland PD2s had the reputation for being fliers provided the route did not require too much gear work on their manual boxes. This is shaping up to be a race down Kingstanding Road on 15 September 1967 and our money is on the Harper bus winning! The BCT bus, 1694 with Brush bodywork, is a veteran dating from 1948 and risks being flagged down by a passenger. The Harper Brothers PD2 is limited stop, moreover it is no 25, a 1962 PD2/28 with Northern Counties 64-seat bodywork, said to be one of the fastest double-deckers in the Birmingham area. Harper Brothers was the largest independent bus operator in Staffordshire when Midland Red took over in 1974. This Leyland became no 2225 in its new owner's fleet and was subsequently cut down to a towing vehicle. It is today preserved by Alex Potts at the Transport Museum Wythall. *Paul Gray/ Transport Museum Wythall*

Above: The 28 was an extraordinary route formed by linking two services. The 22 ran from the city centre south-eastwards to Bolton Road, Small Heath, initially a tramway service until becoming the first to be converted to motorbuses in February 1930. The 21 was an inter-suburban bus service that took in much of the eastern and northern quarters of the city, wandering via Castle Bromwich, Erdington and Kingstanding, terminating in Great Barr. The routes were combined as the 28, the journey length becoming 13.6 miles, longer than the cross-city services, and took 63 minutes each way. The return journey began with this severe climb up Dyas Road, being tackled here by Daimler CVG6 1594, first licensed on 1 January 1948, on a short working to the Fox & Goose. *Geoff Kelland/ MRK collection*

Opposite top: As mentioned on page 14, the Walsall Road services were operated for many years by Midland Red. BCT has provided the Scott Arms stop with a cantilever shelter and fitted the 'lollipop' stop plate on it. Midland Red 2542 was a 1944 Daimler with Brush body that was life extended thanks to a major rebuild by Willowbrook. This included Midland Red's extraordinary requirement for built-up front wings that, if they failed to achieve the desired modernisation, certainly looked purposeful! 2542 originally looked like 2533 on page 125. *Gordon Davies*

Opposite: Still more Midland Red buses along the Walsall Road were introduced on 13 January 1936 to serve the new Beeches Estate. Eventually so many buses were required on the Walsall Road that four Midland Red garages were involved, Bearwood, Digbeth, Sutton Coldfield and Sheepcote Street, giving a wide selection of the company's double-deck stock. The anomalous situation began to be eliminated from 1 September 1957 when the first of three new Birmingham City Transport services, the 52, took over from Midland Red service 188 between Hassop Road, Beeches Estate and the city centre. Midland Red 1951 D5B 3810 is seen on Beeches Road at the junction with Thornbridge Avenue in August 1957. Difficult to imagine anything significant disturbing this pleasant pre-war housing estate but, at the foot of the hill, Beeches Road now has to duck under the thundering M6 motorway, the intrusion visually eased today by tree growth. *F W York/ Transport Museum Wythall*

The area saw many road improvements in the 1960s when the junction with the M6 was constructed just north of the Scott Arms, causing temporary diversions. West Bromwich 1958 Daimler CVG6-30/ Metro-Cammell 218 on its 27 service to the Horns of Queslett is approaching the Scott Arms via Walsall Road instead of Newton Road. The 27 was eventually subsumed in July 1977 under WMPTE into the 453 West Bromwich – Streetly service. 218 is followed by a late model Ford Prefect, the rarer 107E version with 4-speed gearbox, this one gleaming with chromed extras. BCT Fleetline/ Park Royal 3523 heads towards 'Town' on service 51 which had replaced Midland Red's Walsall Road short workings (numbered 119) between the Scott Arms and the city centre from 4 May 1958. *John Carroll/ Transport Museum Wythall*

Hamstead Colliery, Great Barr had an aerial ropeway carried on a lattice viaduct across Hamstead Road. Until the colliery's closure in 1965, the ropeway's trucks took coal waste to be tipped into a worked out quarry. It was easily visible (and audible) from this stop, the commencing point of the cross-city service to Yardley, outside Hamstead's post office. The driver of Crossley-bodied Daimler CVG6 2781 waits for his departure time, leaning on the cast iron green guardian of good timekeeping. The terminus was moved further down the road to a new turning circle in December 1961. *R A Mills/ MRK collection*

BCT's Hamstead terminus was moved in December 1961 a few yards into West Bromwich along Hamstead Road where a turning circle had been constructed. The Bundy clock on view here could well be the same one seen outside the post office in the previous picture. As well as minimising turning and waiting problems on Old Walsall Road, it meant easy transfer to and from West Bromwich's service 6, being worked on 6 April 1968 by no 248, a 1963 Daimler CVG6/ Metro-Cammell. This bus is nowadays preserved at Wythall. West Bromwich adopted the Midland Red and Walsall Corporation style of destination blinds from its 1962 deliveries. *John Carroll/ Transport Museum Wythall*

The only inter-suburban route worked by Birmingham's trams ran between Lozells and Salford Bridge at the foot of Gravelly Hill, nowadays nationally known as Spaghetti Junction, with a few journeys extended to Fort Dunlop. The trams were replaced by buses from 1 October 1950. The replacement buses to Fort Dunlop showed service number 40 with the more numerous Gravelly Hill short workings displaying 40A, renumbered 40E from November 1964. Witton depot had worked the trams, Perry Barr provided the replacing buses. 1951 Daimler CVD6 2746, still wearing wheel appearance discs, stands at Villa Road terminus in September 1953. At this terminus, described as Lozells but actually just within Handsworth, the tram driver simply had to walk from one end of his double-ended vehicle to the other. The replacement buses needed a turning loop that ran via Soho Hill and Hamstead Road. This was changed from 1 August 1971 by relocating the terminus to Piers Road, returning via St Michaels Road. *Transport Museum Wythall*

Public transport between the city centre and Handsworth has a long and interesting history. For example, the horses pulling the trams were not replaced by steam locomotives on the Handsworth route. Instead cable cars ran between Colmore Row and the New Inns from the late 1880s until 1911 when BCT electric tramcars took over. The electric era soon saw a branch tramway opened along Grove Lane to Oxhill Road. The replacing 70 bus service ran further along Oxhill Road to Sandwell Road where Park Royal-bodied Leyland PD2 2189 is turning on 20 September 1967. *Paul Gray/ Transport Museum Wythall*

Going back a generation of Leylands, on 18 September 1950 TD6c no 293, new in 1939, has moved to the loading stop outside the Uplands public house, now demolished. As mentioned earlier, after wartime air raid damage 20 English Electric bodies were purchased unused from Manchester Corporation. 293 was one of the buses damaged in the raid on Hockley garage in 1940. By June 1942 twelve 'Manchester' bodies had been fitted to Leyland TD6c chassis. As the bodies had been intended for Daimlers, fitting them to Leyland chassis was not straightforward and the necessary modifications were carried out by MCW. Adjustments included the front bulkheads, floor bearers, body mounting brackets and rear wheel arch cowls. Chassis alterations were evidently handled at Tyburn Road Works. *R A Mills/ The Bus Archive*

To West Bromwich and beyond

On expiry of the West Bromwich tramway lease in 1924, South Staffs trams to Dudley and Wednesbury were replaced by Birmingham Corporation trams running well beyond the city boundary under a 15-year operating agreement. Motor buses took over on 2 April 1939, this time operated jointly by BCT and West Bromwich Corporation. The services comprised the 74 to Dudley, 75 to Wednesbury and their short workings. West Bromwich Corporation began 1957 with 12 new Daimler CVG6 buses, 187-98. These differed in having 60-seat bodies by Willowbrook, a builder enjoying some success with operators in the area around this time. No 191 passes through Hockley, with its new flyover, on an inbound journey on 14 April 1969. BCT's Hockley garage on Whitmore Street can be seen in the background. *Malcolm Keeley*

The boundary between Birmingham and West Bromwich offered not only the West Bromwich Albion football ground and the delicious aroma of Bradford's Bakery but also a car checkover for seven shillings (35p). The largest batch of buses delivered to West Bromwich after World War Two were twenty 1952 Daimler CVG6 like no 161 here. The Metro-Cammell half of the MCW organization normally handled the West Bromwich body contracts but, on this occasion, the 56-seat bodies were provided by the other partner, Weymann. *Paul Gray/ Transport Museum Wythall*

Opposite top: West Bromwich's original 1939 tram replacement buses were Daimler COG6 models with Metro-Cammell 56-seat bodies like no 92 here. Thirty were needed for the Birmingham services, including maintenance spares, plus a few more for other routes. This large intake into a relatively small fleet meant their replacement had to be spread over several years. Some COG6s were therefore rebuilt to extend their lives; they were gradually taken out of service between 1956 and 1963. West Bromwich Corporation ran a tight organisation permitting very low fares. The buses operated out of Oak Lane garage, opened in 1930 and extended to accommodate the 1939 increase in fleet. This also housed other council-owned vehicles such as ambulances, refuse wagons, parks vehicles and staff cars. Buses were available for maintenance between the peaks while other vehicles occupied staff during the rush periods, maximising efficiency. *Transport Museum Wythall*

Opposite bottom: Situated beyond West Bromwich, Wednesbury sounds a long way from the centre of Brum. In fact the 75 service between Birmingham Snow Hill and Wednesbury was 7.6 miles and took 38 minutes each way, barely longer than some radial services entirely within the Birmingham boundary. This is one of those parts of the Black Country that have changed immensely in the last half century. BCT Park Royal-bodied Leyland PD2 2194 climbs from the centre of Wednesbury up Holloway Bank. In the tramway era when the weather was snowy or icy, the first tram of the day would descend this hill on the upward track to ease its passage on the return journey. *R Mallabon/ Transport Museum Wythall*

Above: The terminus of the 75 in Wednesbury was the White Horse, now demolished. Buses of all four municipal bus operators absorbed into WMPTE in 1969 could be seen here. Across the road in August 1957 from BCT's Crossley-bodied Daimler CVG6 3178 and a 1949 all-Leyland PD2 is a Walsall Corporation Guy Arab III with Park Royal body working the Walsall – Darlaston - Wednesbury - Walsall circular. *F W York/ Transport Museum Wythall*

The 74 Birmingham Snow Hill – Dudley service was 9.6 miles and took 47 minutes each way, terminating in Dudley's bus station after its opening in September 1952. Previously the 74 buses had terminated, like the trams they replaced, at Dudley railway station at the bottom of the hill. Passengers no longer had to wheeze their way uphill to the shops and markets, alighting instead at this set-down stop on the notorious gradient in Birmingham Street. All-Leyland PD2 2136 waves the BCT flag but Midland Red buses dominated here. A BMMO D7 loads on the left while, in the background, a GD6 class Guy Arab III turns left. *Michael Dryhurst*

This is the Fisher Street loading stop in Dudley which was thankfully more or less on the flat. BCT Park Royal-bodied Leyland PD2 2189 will work the departure after West Bromwich Weymann-bodied Daimler 164 in March 1962. The rear of 2189 is nicely rounded, spoiled only by the coachbuilder's standard flat upper deck emergency window. *F W York/ Transport Museum Wythall*